Warp Speed

changes taking place and why they happened. Anyone concerned with how well we as a profession are now using our priceless freedoms—many of them expanded in the 1960s at great sacrifice and endangered today because of the recklessness with which they are being employed—would do well to read their description of the decline of the editing function, and of the rise of a culture of allegation and assertion at the expense of an older culture of verification. For that delineation alone, as well as many of the other important points they make, we are very much in their debt.

Bill Kovach and Tom Rosenstiel

WARP SPEED

America in the Age of Mixed Media

A CENTURY FOUNDATION BOOK

1999 ◆ The Century Foundation Press ◆ New York

The Century Foundation, formerly the Twentieth Century Fund, sponsors and supervises timely analyses of economic policy, foreign affairs, and domestic political issues. Not-for-profit and nonpartisan, it was founded in 1919 and endowed by Edward A. Filene.

LIBRARY OF CONGRESS CATALOGING-IN-PUBLICATION DATA

Kovach, Bill.
Warp Speed : America in the age of mixed media / Bill Kovach and Tom Rosenstiel.
p. cm.
"A Century Foundation book."
Includes bibliographical references (p.) and index.
ISBN 0–87078–436–6. -- ISBN 0–87078–437–4
1. Press and politics--United States. 2. Journalism--Political aspects--United States. 3. United States--Politics and government--1993- I. Rosenstiel, Tom. II. Title.
PN4888.P6K68 1999
070.4'49324'0973--dc21 99-20700
CIP

Cover Design and Artwork: Claude Goodwin
Manufactured in the United States of America.

FOREWORD

At century's end, most of us have developed an elaborate, though sometimes unconscious, set of skills designed to deal with the complexity of modern life. With regard to information, we are fairly ruthless editors, opening ourselves only to a very small fraction of the tidal wave of messages available. Recognizing that it is impractical to sample everything, we bring a semblance of order to our choices through habits that determine what we look for and to whom we listen.

In terms of understanding the great public events of our time, most of us turn to others to do much of the editing for us: the newspaper or the evening television broadcast, for example, as well as less formal sources such as knowledgeable (or, at least, voluble) co-workers, family members, or neighbors. We settle, in short, on familiar sources, if not the most reputable ones.

The choices we make of sources spell the difference between financial and professional success or failure for those in the business of winning our trust—or, at least, attracting our attention. The most responsible of those vying to provide us information seek to win our allegiance by offering the best available version of the truth. And, while news outlets can and do decide to withhold or delay an item because it does not meet their internally established standards of reliability, in a competitive environment even the most responsible news organizations or reporters always have felt pressure to produce on deadline. Thus, just as the public compromises by relying on secondary sources of information, news organizations sometimes must settle for a reasonably justifiable facsimile of reality—something well short of truth itself. On big stories, with lots at stake, the process has never been easy or error free. But in recent years, the decisions about what to go with and when have become increasingly complex and controversial.

The news media today operate in an environment that would have been unimaginable just a generation ago. In the first place, we are, depending on your point of view, either a coarser nation or a more candid one—or both. We have become accustomed to talking with strangers about matters that formerly were out-of-bounds even with one's best friends and family. Consequently, the news media cannot ignore the fact that there is simply much more that is considered "fit to print." Second, the proliferation of media outlets and the more competitive market environment in which they operate have altered the internal dynamics of virtually all aspects of journalism. Third, the changes encompassed by the so-called twenty-four-hour news cycle and the appearance of remarkably unfiltered items of information on the Internet have transformed both the time scale and the standards for what is news. Together, these developments have blurred the line between mainstream news and unsupported gossip. They have made the sensational—however unsubstantiated—acceptable.

All these elements and more came together in the White House scandal involving the president's liaison with an office intern. That story is all too well known and most of us have heard more than enough. Still, the questions that the scandal illuminated about the present state of the news business are interesting and important in their own right. Indeed, in the hands of two of journalism's most thoughtful practitioners, Bill Kovach, the curator of the Nieman Foundation for Journalism at Harvard University, and Tom Rosenstiel, director of the Project for Excellence in Journalism, the events of the past eighteen months provide a telling case study of the toughest issues confronting the profession today.

Throughout the 1990s, The Century Foundation has called attention to the rapidly evolving changes in the relationships among the news media, the government, and the public. Our Perspectives on the News series of reports were ahead of the curve in highlighting the seeds of alarming developments that blossomed during the coverage of the Monica Lewinsky episode. Perhaps most prescient was a 1992 report titled *The New News v. the Old News* by Jay Rosen and Paul Taylor, which was among the first publications to detect the declining dominance of elite media institutions in influencing public perceptions about the news. Among the related books The Century Foundation has sponsored, Lawrence K. Grossman's *The Electronic Republic: Reshaping Democracy in the Information Age* anticipated the enormous impact of the Internet, which plays such an important role in the story told here.

Warp Speed is the first book to synthesize and put into perspective the ways in which the public learned about the Lewinsky scandal and events related to the president's impeachment. Even more importantly, it assesses the likely long-term fallout for journalism and public discourse while putting forward some ideas for limiting excesses that serve no one's interests. We are grateful to Kovach and Rosenstiel for their thoughtful analysis of this difficult and important issue.

RICHARD C. LEONE, *PRESIDENT*
The Century Foundation
March 1999

PREFACE

by David Halberstam

The past year has been, I think, the worst year for American journalism since I entered the profession forty-four years ago. It is not that journalists—if in fact it is journalists who have been covering the Monica Lewinsky-Clinton-Starr story—are unpopular. Traditionally, when reporters do their best work they are almost always unpopular: they tend to be ahead of the societal curve and more often than not they are the bearers of news that jars conventional sensibilities and attitudes. So it was during much of the civil rights story, so it was during Vietnam, and so it was for much of the early going during Watergate. What is disturbing about the bad odor of journalism today is that, I think, many of the critics are right, and the people who have been performing as journalists in the past year have in fact seriously trivialized the profession, often doing what is fashionable instead of what is right. Very simply, like many of my colleagues, I think that the proportion of coverage given the story—compared to the rest of the news budget—is hopelessly out of synch, and that the standards for verifications, so critical to serious and fair reporting, have fallen dramatically.

In some ways this particular crisis, so much of it driven by technological change, has been coming for more than a decade, as the power of cable television and the effect of it on mainstream media have gradually changed the nature of what constitutes television broadcasting, giving us an ever escalating diet of sensationalized tabloid reporting, and an endless, unquestioning search for access to celebrities on their own terms. It was simply that in the past year this new media culture reached deeper into the nation's bloodstream, and more traditional barriers were dropped at ever higher levels of the profession.

Somewhere, gradually but systematically, there has been an abdication of responsibility within the profession, most particularly at the networks. Television's gatekeepers, at a time when a fragmenting audience threatens the singular profits of the past, stopped being gatekeepers. The historic definition of a great editor—someone who balances what people want to know with what they *need* to know—has been deftly jettisoned. Lines between reporting and being a pundit have been blurred, without penalty.

Some of the changes obviously began with the rise of cable television and its tabloid news shows, which the networks with their declining audiences soon felt a need to respond to and emulate. Some of them are the by-product of a twenty-four-hour news cycle in which the capacity of editors to make balanced judgments on what constitutes news is inevitably in decline—the technology simply overwhelms the people working on the desks. The magazine shows—if that is the word—produced by the networks as their answer to the cable shows reflect little about a complicated nation and world (the implosion of the post-Cold War Russia, the crisis of class in America caused by the changing nature of an economy that offers ever greater rewards at the top and smaller ones at the middle and at the bottom). The great new sin in television news is not to be inaccurate, it is to be boring.

Talk shows, allegedly public affairs oriented, desperate for even the smallest share of a fractured market, have become ever more confrontational—anxious, it would seem, to shed heat instead of light. For many traditional journalists, this has been the most disheartening of years—we barely recognize what we thought was our own profession and the values now at play; it is a world where television's executive gatekeepers seem to look the other way on ethical questions, and where signature on-air figures of network television have made their own varying degrees of accommodation to the onslaught of the new media.

In this extremely painful year, Bill Kovach and Tom Rosenstiel have been particularly vigilant in trying to articulate the enduring values so much under assault. Now in this small but valuable and thoughtful book, they have outlined with great skill and lucidity the

Contents

1

THE JOURNALISM OF ASSERTION

Marshall McLuhan was wrong. If the medium really were the message, Americans would always elect the most able television communicator. Pat Buchanan would have beaten George Bush. Richard Nixon might have been commissioner of baseball but never president.

That, however, is not how America operates. In the fifty years since television became a force in politics, only two masters of the medium have been elected leader of the country—Ronald Reagan and John Kennedy. Arguably, Bill Clinton might be a third. Buchanan's skills on television take him only so far. His ideas, while they energize some voters, alienate others. Much the same is true for another gifted communicator, Jesse Jackson. Citizens weigh countless factors in making their decisions, including ideology. The most clever ads often do not correlate into votes.[1] The message, not the medium, is the message after all.

No doubt the medium and the media shape what messages are sent and how they are put together. But how, and how much? To what extent does the culture of news define our politics? The principal focus of this work is to examine the contours of the new media culture, which we call the Mixed Media Culture, and to explain its effect on contemporary political debate.

That task is made more difficult—and more necessary—because the culture of news is changing so rapidly. Journalism is in a state of disorientation brought on by rapid technological change, declining market share, and growing pressure to operate with economic efficiency. In a sometimes desperate search to reclaim audience, the press has moved more toward sensationalism, entertainment, and opinion. In only the last year, journalism has suffered a host of embarrassments over press ethics and still further declines in audience size and public confidence, and has engaged in new levels of self-examination. No event signals the changing norms as much as the Clinton–Lewinsky scandal that led to the impeachment proceedings against William Jefferson Clinton. To that degree, this work will try to understand the new media culture through that event.

The ordeal of Monica Lewinsky, Bill Clinton, Kenneth Starr, and the impeachment trial they precipitated were part of a kind of cultural civil war in America in which the press plays a peculiarly important role. As a consequence, this work will also try to assess the role of the press in contributing to that growing conflict that has gripped politics over the last several decades. Finally, this work will attempt to offer some modest suggestions for how journalists might try to cope with this new Mixed Media Culture of news.

At least in its broadest outlines, the sex scandal involving Clinton was not unprecedented. In the summer of 1964, high-ranking law enforcement officials armed with secret tape transcripts made the rounds to selected journalists in Washington. The tapes had conclusive evidence that one of the nation's most respected and powerful political figures was cheating on his wife.

When the transcripts weren't enough, no less a figure than the director of the Federal Bureau of Investigation got involved directly. J. Edgar Hoover invited some reporters to FBI headquarters to actually listen to the tapes themselves. There, you can hear it. He's having sex there. Out of wedlock. Adulterer.

The man caught on the tapes was controversial in his own right. A minister. A man who used the Bible in nearly every speech. A man whose primary tactic was to use guilt, morality, and an appeal to goodness as forces for persuasion. To Hoover, the hypocrisy was overwhelming; it was proof that Martin Luther King, Jr. could be considered a fraud and a hypocrite. This is precisely the kind of criticism of officials that journalists in the 1990s feel they are obliged to make.

Hoover's intent was to "expose" King, the FBI director said,[2] to "disrupt, misdirect, discredit or otherwise neutralize" the black leader.

Not one reporter wrote a story, even those friendly to Hoover and unfriendly to King. Evidence of the campaign against King and the direct use of the tapes did not emerge for nearly two decades.

How different would American history be had the press operated differently in 1964? It is impossible, of course, to place the behavior of a political figure from one period into the context of another period, or impose the judgments of one time on those of another. Perhaps King would have behaved differently.

But imagine Hoover sharing his tapes with professional Internet gossip Matt Drudge. How would CNN handle the leaked tapes if the network knew MSNBC was about to be given the same information? Would rumor of King's extramarital activities be "Issue One" on the *McLaughlin Group?* Or ferried into a debate on talk radio or *Crossfire?* What would the attorney general have done if a special prosecutor were investigating evidence Hoover was peddling of King connections with the Communist party, and King were asked under oath about adultery?

Harris Wofford, the former Pennsylvania senator who had known King since the early 1950s, first wrote about Hoover's efforts in 1980 in *Of Kennedys and Kings*. He believes that in the media culture of the 1990s, one of the most important Americans of the twentieth century would have been destroyed and American history would have been quite different.[3]

Bill Clinton is not Martin Luther King, and Kenneth Starr is not J. Edgar Hoover. The King incident did not involve a lawsuit, a special prosecutor, or allegations of perjury and obstruction of justice. Nor was King an elected official. But the basic issue of what the press is willing to publish today compared with a generation ago is unmistakable. And no doubt it matters.

While the press may not tell people what to think, it gives them a list of things to think about. In so doing the news culture still shapes the lines of the political playing field and the context in which citizens define meaning for political events. The rules of the political and media culture alter not only how politics is conducted, but increasingly who participates, why, and the nature of what can be accomplished.

The Lewinsky story did not change everything in the American media culture. Instead, it represented a convergence of long-standing trends, which came together with the political culture and clarified in part the consequences of both.

To understand these changes, it is helpful to recognize what the Clinton scandal represented for the press: the moment when the new post-O.J. media culture turned its camera lens to a major political event for the first time. What do we mean by the post-O.J. media culture? It is a newly diversified mass media in which the cultures of entertainment, infotainment, argument, analysis, tabloid, and mainstream press not only work side by side but intermingle and merge. It is a culture in which Matt Drudge sits alongside William Safire on *Meet the Press* and Ted Koppel talks about the nuances of oral sex, in which *Hard Copy* and CBS News jostle for camera position outside the federal grand jury to hear from a special prosecutor.

Previous major political scandals such as Iran-Contra predated this merging of news cultures. Other recent incidents such as Gennifer Flowers were too fleeting to offer more than a glimpse of the new world of competition that batters down the very notion of journalist as gatekeeper. After Monica and Bill, the cultures were merged into one, not merely in the minds of a distracted public but in fact. NBC News owned MSNBC, which merged its own identity with the Clinton scandal. Its *Meet the Press* program turned Internet gossip pamphleteer Matt Drudge into a pundit, and Fox News made him into a TV show host. *Newsweek* reporter Mike Isikoff covers the story for *Newsweek* and is under contract with MSNBC and NBC to offer punditry about it—to the delight of his managers at *Newsweek*, which encourages reporters to become pundits and pays them for each radio and TV appearance. From *NBC Nightly News* to MSNBC's "The Crisis in The White House" to *Dateline*'s infotainment as journalism to Matt Drudge—the line is more blurred than the Mixed Media Culture likes to admit.

We will base our critique of the Mixed Media Culture on a variety of work we conducted throughout 1998 in our positions as chairman and vice chairman of the Committee of Concerned Journalists, a group of reporters, editors, producers, publishers, and educators concerned about the direction of the craft. This work included three major content studies of the Clinton scandal coverage, as well as three public forums we sponsored involving key journalists who covered the story. We will also draw on numerous interviews we conducted throughout the year with journalists inside and outside of Washington.

We will argue that in the new Mixed Media Culture the classic function of journalism to sort out a true and reliable account of the day's events is being undermined. It is being displaced by the continuous news cycle, the growing power of sources over reporters, varying standards of journalism, and a fascination with inexpensive, polarizing argument. The press is also increasingly fixated on finding the "big story" that will temporarily reassemble the now-fragmented mass audience. Yet these same characteristics are only serving to deepen the disconnection with citizens, diminish the press's ability to serve as a cohesive cultural force, and weaken the public's tether to a true account of the news. The long-term implications for the role the Founders saw as most important for the press—that of being a forum for public debate and as such a catalyst for problem solving—is being eroded.

The way in which the new Mixed Media Culture has diluted the stream of accurate and reliable information with innuendo and pseudofacts had an impact on the Clinton scandal. It partly explains why the impeachment left so many Americans estranged, as if it were a TV show rather than a political crisis. The notion that author Daniel Boorstin introduced in *The Image* in 1961, in which what was true was becoming less important than what one could make seem true, had thoroughly saturated the political culture by the late 1990s. Politicians had created an environment in which lying became respectable by calling it *spin*. They invented "doctors" to administer it. The effect was acute. Pointing out one of the principal differences between the Watergate scandal and the Clinton scandal, journalist Benjamin C. Bradlee observed, "People lie now in a way that they never lied before—and the ease with which they lie, the total ease. . . . People expect no consequences. . . . This word *spinning* . . . is a nice uptown way of saying lying." That was at the heart of the disconnect of the Clinton impeachment: a political establishment that had so perfected and celebrated dissembling lacked the authority with the public to evince outrage and try to convict someone for lying. The irony of it was manifestly plain to most Americans, but it was largely missed inside Washington.

During the Clinton scandal, the press, the group with the biggest stake in maintaining the integrity of facts and accuracy, further succumbed to the ethos of pseudofacts. The Mixed Media now elevate to the status of celebrities, and in some cases embrace as journalists, the same spin doctors and dissemblers—people like George Stephanopoulos or Tony Blankley—once paid to manipulate them. They create pseudoexperts, people who look good but have limited expertise, to appear on their talk shows. They create news networks without reporters, relying instead on argument to pass as journalism. In the process, the Mixed Media Culture contributes to the blending of fact and assertion, real events and pseudoevents, news and entertainment—what journalist Richard Reeves has called "the Oliver Stoning of America."[4]

The new Mixed Media Culture has five main characteristics:

- *A Never-Ending News Cycle Makes Journalism Less Complete:* In the continuous news cycle, the press is increasingly oriented toward ferrying allegations rather than first ferreting out the truth. Stories often come as piecemeal bits of evidence, accusation, or speculation—to be filled in and sorted out in public as the day progresses. The initiating charge is quickly aired. Then journalists vamp and speculate until the response is issued. The demand of keeping up with and airing the to and fro leaves journalists with less time to take stock and sort out beforehand what is genuinely significant. Ironically, it means the news is delivered less completely. This gives the reporting a more chaotic, unsettled, and even numbing quality. It can make tuning in to the news seem inefficient. It also makes it more difficult to separate fact from spin, argument, or innuendo, and makes the culture significantly more susceptible to manipulation.

- *Sources Are Gaining Power Over Journalists:* The move toward allegation over verification is compounded by a shift in the power relationship toward the sources of information and away from the news organizations who cover them. Sources increasingly dictate the terms of the interaction and the conditions and time frame in which information is used, and set the ground rules for their anonymity. They shop stories from outlet to outlet, striking bargains to their own best advantage, whether it is a celebrity trying to promote a new movie or a leaker negotiating which newspaper or prime time magazine to give the interview to. This shift in leverage toward those who would manipulate the press is partly a function of intensifying economic competition among a proliferating number of news outlets—a matter of a rising demand for news product and a limited supply of news makers. It is also a function of the growing sophistication in the art of media manipulation.

- *There Are No More Gatekeepers:* The proliferation of outlets diminishes the authority of any one outlet to play a gatekeeper role over the information it publishes. One of the key features of the Mixed Media Culture is that the press is now marked by a much wider range of standards of what is publishable and what is not. On one hand, journalism is richer, more democratic, more innovative, and, given the possibility of narrower targeting of audiences, has the potential of becoming closer to its audience. On the other hand, the loss of market share, fragmentation of revenue, and disorientation has meant an abandonment of professional standards and ethics. Information is moving so fast, news outlets are caught between trying to gather the information for citizens and interpreting what others have delivered ahead of them. In practice, the lowest standards tend to drive out the higher, creating a kind of Gresham's Law of Journalism. What does the news organization that requires high levels of substantiation do with the reports of those with lesser levels of proof?

- *Argument Is Overwhelming Reporting:* The reporting culture (which rewards gathering and verifying information) is being increasingly overrun by what Deborah Tannen has called the "argument culture," which devalues the science of verification. The information revolution is a prime force behind the rise of the argument culture. Many of the new media outlets are engaged in commenting on information rather than gathering it. The rise of twenty-four-hour news stations and Internet news and information sites has placed demands on the press to "have something" to fill the time. The economics of these new media, indeed, demand that this product be produced as cheaply as possible. Commentary, chat, speculation, opinion, argument, controversy, and punditry cost far less than assembling a team of reporters, producers, fact checkers, and editors to cover the far-flung corners of the world. Whole new news organizations such as MSNBC are being built around such chatter, creating a new medium of talk radio TV.

- *The "Blockbuster Mentality":* As the audience for news fragments, outlets such as network television that depend on a mass audience are increasingly interested in stories that temporarily reassemble the mass media audience. These big stories might be analogous to a hit movie or song that crosses over traditional audience divisions, and their appeal creates a "Summer Blockbuster" mentality in the media. These blockbusters tend to be formulaic stories that involve celebrity, scandal, sex, and downfall, be it O.J., Diana, or Monicagate. Part of their appeal to news organizations is it is cheaper and easier to reassemble the audience with the big story than by covering the globe and presenting a diversified menu of news.

These new characteristics of the Mixed Media Culture are creating what we call a new journalism of assertion, which is less interested in substantiating whether something is true and more interested in getting it into the public discussion. The journalism of assertion contributes to the press being a conduit of politics as cultural civil war. The combatants in that war can employ the piecemeal nature of news and the weakened leverage of the gatekeepers to exploit the varying standards of different news organizations. These combatants also flourish amid the growing reliance on polarized argument. The role the press has played in the fight over values is not new. Television is well suited to symbolic, polarizing issues. And the growing heterogeneity of the press, while it more accurately reflects the diverse interests of the audience, makes it difficult for the press to find cultural common ground.

The solution, to the extent that one can be identified, is not in trying to enforce a lost homogeneity on journalism. Rather, it is in individual news organizations becoming more clear-headed and courageous about what their own purpose and standards are, and then sticking to them.

Those who fare best in this new culture, at least in classic journalistic terms, are those who do their own research. These news outlets are governed by their own internal standards because they are having to make their own judgments about when a story is verified, what is true, and what is relevant. They are less susceptible to repeating others' mistakes, and they are most careful about accuracy because they bear sole and original responsibility.

Increasingly, news organizations will be forced to distinguish themselves not by the speed and accuracy of their reporting, their depth, or even the quality of their interpretation. The perpetual news cycle will synthesize virtually all news reporting and interpretation into a kind of blended mix. Scoops remain exclusive for only a matter of seconds. Instead, news organizations will have to distinguish and establish their brand by the values and standards they bring to the news. When and how do they use anonymous sources? Will they publish charges they cannot substantiate simply because others have? When is someone's private life publicly relevant? This means news organizations should do more to think through in advance what their news values and policies are on a variety of key journalistic matters. And as newspapers did a century ago, in a time of similar intense competition, they will do well to articulate and market themselves to the public according to those values.

Whether traditional news values—such as verification, proportion, and relevance—survive depends ultimately on whether they matter to the public. News outlets that aspire to high standards on such matters as proof of accuracy and proportionality distinguish themselves by more than self-censorship. They offer the public reliability and save people time. In a world with growing choices, and one where the depth of information is potentially infinite for every user, the highest value may be given to the source whose information is most accurate, most dependable, and most efficient to use.

In the end, the importance of having an accurate, reliable account of events is profound. "Public as well as private reason depends on it," Walter Lippmann noted eighty years ago. "Not what somebody says, not what somebody wishes were true, but what is so, beyond all our opinion, constitutes the touchstone of our sanity."[5]

The question before us now is whether the search for what is so, the journalism of verification, will be soon overwhelmed by the new journalism of assertion.

2

WHAT HAPPENED?

Shortly after midnight on Saturday, January 17, Linda Tripp's lawyer arrived at the Washington offices of *Newsweek* with two tape recordings. *Newsweek* correspondent Michael Isikoff had been working for months with Tripp and her friend Lucianne Goldberg on a story about President Bill Clinton having an affair with a former White House intern named Monica Lewinsky.[1] Over the previous five days, according to the most detailed accounts of the story, Goldberg and Tripp had set a variety of events in motion, plotting what Tripp would say to Lewinsky on the tapes, trying to get Isikoff to write about the alleged affair, and when that still wasn't enough, contacting Kenneth Starr's office. When *Newsweek* hesitated, in part because Starr was now trying to get *Newsweek* to delay, Tripp's lawyer arranged for them to hear the tapes for themselves.

After hearing the tapes, evaluating what they had, and weighing Starr's entreaties that it wait a week, *Newsweek* decided against running the story—in part in exchange for a promise from Starr's office of a complete account for the following week's magazine.[2]

Shortly after midnight, about five hours after *Newsweek* decided to hold off on the story, Matt Drudge—the one-man Internet gossip and news agency—was tipped off about the piece, and decided the public had a right to know even if the facts couldn't be verified. He posted a version of the story on his Web page. *Newsweek* editors maintain they do not know for certain how the story found its way into Drudge's hands. Their suspicions, however, center on Goldberg, Tripp's book agent. Isikoff had informed her Saturday evening of *Newsweek*'s decision to hold off. Drudge's Internet account that night claimed *Newsweek* had decided to "spike" the story, but that thanks to him the information was being made public:

> At the last minute, at 6 P.M. on Saturday evening, *Newsweek* magazine killed a story that was destined to shake official Washington to its foundation: A White House intern carried on a sexual affair with the President of the United States!
>
> The *DRUDGE REPORT* has learned that reporter Michael Isikoff developed the story of his career, only to have it spiked by top *Newsweek* suits hours before publication. A young woman, twenty-three, sexually involved with the love of her life, the President of the United States, since she was a 21-year-old intern at the White House. . . .
>
> Michael Isikoff was not available for comment late Saturday. *Newsweek* was on voice mail.
>
> The White House was busy checking the *DRUDGE REPORT* for details.

The next day Drudge's account came up during the roundtable segment of ABC's *This Week with Sam Donaldson and Cokie Roberts*. The *Weekly Standard*'s Bill Kristol floated the story and quickly found himself under attack.

> *Bill Kristol:* I also think the media—you mentioned the media—is going to be an issue here. The story in Washington this morning is that *Newsweek* magazine was going to go with a big story based on tape-recorded conversations, which a woman who was a summer intern at the White House, an intern of Leon Panetta's. . . .
>
> *George Stephanopoulos:* And Bill, where did it come from? The Drudge Report. You know, we've all seen how discredited . . .
>
> *Bill Kristol:* No, no, no. They had screaming arguments in *Newsweek* Magazine yesterday. They finally didn't go with the story. It's going to be a question of whether the media is now going to report what are pretty well-validated charges of presidential behavior in the White House.

Sam Donaldson: I'm not an apologist for *Newsweek*, but if their editors decided they didn't have it cold enough to go with, I don't think that we can here without—unless you've seen what they were basing their decision on—how could we say *Newsweek* was wrong to kill it.

What difference such a conversation makes is difficult to assess. In the culture of Washington journalism, the Sunday talk shows are closely watched for internal buzz as much as for important news. Since the introduction of the *Washington Post* Style section in the late 1960s, Washington power struggles have been as much about the gossip of Washington as the work of Washington. David Brinkley once called them the political establishment's "intercom."[3] Transcripts of the programs are faxed to every news bureau on understaffed Sunday afternoons. Reporters on Monday knew that Drudge had reported that *Newsweek* had killed the story—Kristol had mentioned it on *This Week*. Aides in Starr's office knew that the story was breaking into the news media. On Monday, Drudge's e-mail was in the hands of a variety of influential news managers who subscribe, such as Doyle McManus, the Washington bureau chief of the *Los Angeles Times*.

If the people in Starr's office were reluctant to talk on Saturday, they were more willing to do so after all this. In the early evening of Tuesday, January 20, the investigative reporter at the *LA Times* covering Whitewater, Dave Willman, walked into McManus's office. Wilman told the bureau chief that Independent Counsel Kenneth Starr just had his mandate broadened to look into allegations of the affair and whether Clinton had told Lewinsky to lie and committed perjury. *Times* reporters immediately went to work on the story and found they weren't alone with the scoop. "The *Washington Post* had the story the same evening, ABC News had the story the same evening," McManus says. "So, there was clearly a lot of leakage."[4]

Late Tuesday night, the story hit the mainstream. In its early edition, the *Washington Post* announced "CLINTON ACCUSED OF URGING AIDE TO LIE; STARR PROBES WHETHER PRESIDENT TOLD WOMAN TO DENY ALLEGED AFFAIR TO JONES'S LAWYERS" across four columns on the front page. The attribution for their account was, "Sources close to the investigation." Only minutes after midnight, ABC News had broadcast a story recapping the *Post* story on its radio network. And the *Los Angeles Times* also broke the story in its Wednesday paper with a page 1 piece, "STARR EXAMINES CLINTON LINK TO FEMALE INTERN."

The speed with which the Lewinsky story now moved was breathtaking. By Wednesday afternoon, only a few hours after it first broke, Scripps Howard News Service was reporting that one person who had heard the Lewinsky tapes said the former intern "described how Clinton allegedly first urged her to have oral sex, telling her that such acts were not technically adultery." By Wednesday evening, ABC, CBS, and NBC, all broadcasting from Cuba where the Pope was set to arrive, led with the story. In prime time, the allegations were the focus of *Larry King Live* and *Rivera Live!* as well as specials on CNN and MSNBC.

By Wednesday night, the first day of the story, *Nightline*'s Ted Koppel solemnly looked into the camera and proclaimed that Clinton's crisis "may come down to the question of whether oral sex does or does not constitute adultery."

On Day Two, the story accelerated. Both Matt Drudge and Michael Isikoff appeared on the *Today Show* at different times to discuss the story. Drudge, in his interview, announced, "There's a potential DNA trail that would tie Clinton to this young woman." The day before his Web site had announced the potential existence of a semen-stained dress. It was the first mention of the alleged piece of evidence that would later become significant in the story. And in Havana, TV anchors Tom Brokaw, Peter Jennings, and Dan Rather all packed up and headed home. By Thursday evening, Brokaw and Rather were in Washington and Jennings in New York.

On Friday ABC News announced, "a source with direct knowledge of Lewinsky's allegations" had information about when the Clinton–Lewinsky rendezvous took place. Furthermore, the source told ABC's Jackie Judd that Lewinsky had kept a blue dress stained with the president's semen as a "kind of souvenir."

By Sunday, January 25, the tapes few had heard were the focus of the *Washington Post* story that discussed in detail their contents, like "an eighteen-month involvement that included late-night trysts at the White House featuring oral sex." The *Post*'s source? "Descriptions of key discussions recorded on the tapes" that the paper had received from "sources who have listened to portions of them." The Sunday talk shows focused almost solely on the allegations. The possibilities of impeachment or resignation were a major topic of discussion. ABC announced another major scoop. "Several sources" had told Jackie

Judd that Starr was looking into claims that the president and Lewinsky were caught in an intimate encounter by Secret Service agents or White House staffers.

Television pundits were quick to make predictions that simultaneously changed the stakes and the political landscape for the president. On Wednesday, the day the story first broke, Tim Russert, speaking on MSNBC, said, "One of his best friends told me today, 'If this is true he has got to get out of town.' Whether it will come to that, I don't know, and I don't think it's fair to play the speculation game. But I do not underestimate anything happening at this point. The next forty-eight to seventy-two hours are crucial."[5]

On Sunday, Sam Donaldson said Clinton might have to resign within a week: "If he's not telling the truth, I think his presidency is numbered in days. This isn't going to drag out. . . . If he's not telling the truth, the evidence shows [Mr. Clinton] will resign, perhaps this week."[6]

Almost as quick as the velocity of the story was the speed of the backlash of the coverage.

"Has there ever been a more disgusting media meltdown?" *New York Times* columnist Russell Baker wrote. "The President is alleged to have had illicit sexual relations with a younger woman and—stop the presses!—it's Armageddon time."[7]

As we will see, there is some evidence to suggest that the Lewinsky story did not represent a sea change for journalism as much as a culmination—and acceleration—of trends evolving over two decades.

"Are there new rules of journalism and a new journalistic culture?" asked Tom Patterson of Harvard's Shorenstein Center.[8] "The tendencies that we see in news today, the reliance on unnamed and anonymous sources, the insertions of journalists' opinions, scholars began to recognize these tendencies in the news in the late 1970s and they've increased with time."

This distinction is important, for it reveals that the story was not an anomaly but a reflection of deeper shifts influencing the culture of news and politics.

To understand what those shifts are, however, and what they mean, we need to see precisely what occurred in the breaking days of Lewinsky, by the numbers.

3

The Parameters of the Mixed Media Culture

In the third week of the Clinton–Lewinsky story, amid growing concerns of declining standards, the Committee of Concerned Journalists—an ad hoc group of journalists who had formed several months before—commissioned a study to find out precisely what the press had reported in the first week of the story, what the sourcing was, and how much was actual reporting versus commentary and opinion.

The study's most important finding was the extraordinary degree to which reporting and opinion and speculation were now intermingled in mainstream journalism. A snapshot of network news, newspaper reporting, and cable news that typified what an American might see showed that a remarkable 41 percent of all the reportage in the first six days of the Clinton–Lewinsky story was not factual reporting at all—here is what happened—but was instead journalists offering their own analysis, opinion, speculation, or judgments—essentially commentary and punditry.[1] Another 12 percent of reportage was reporting attributed to other news organizations and unverified by the outlet now repeating it. Taken together, that means that more than half of the reportage in the first week (53 percent) of this story was either passing along other people's reporting or commenting on the news.[2] While we know of no other story that has been analyzed quite this way to offer a statistical comparison, we think it is fair to assume that such levels of commentary and repetition of others' work are unprecedented. The number of talk shows has exploded, and the speed of new technology has dramatically increased the ability and the inclination to pass on what others are reporting without independently verifying it.

What this reveals is the degree to which the supposed information revolution is not actually about gathering information but instead about commenting on information that others have gathered. The effects of this shift toward interpretation, or the "argument culture," would permeate coverage of the Clinton–Lewinsky story. The argument culture, which we will discuss at more length later, is one in which discussions are framed around polarized extremes and are designed to raise the ire of participants and citizens. In this culture, facts are often subordinated to emotion and common ground is subordinated to conflict. Problem solving becomes more difficult.

The study also cataloged what the press was reporting in that first week. Six assertions or allegations dominated the coverage. The most common was that Clinton was in big trouble. The second was that Clinton was denying there was any sexual relationship. The third was that Lewinsky had alleged sex and perjury. The fourth was that Lewinsky was negotiating immunity. The fifth was that Clinton was dissembling. The sixth was that impeachment was a possibility.

Interestingly, three of the six most common assertions in the press that first week were essentially subjective or interpretative: that this spelled big trouble, that Clinton was not telling the truth, and that impeachment was a possibility. Within a few weeks, each of those interpretations looked to be premature or false. In time, however, the story would regain political momentum, and these prophecies came true.

If the press rushed to judgment in the first week, it did appear to calm down somewhat over time. A second study by the Committee of Concerned Journalists, monitoring coverage six weeks into the story, found that the level of punditry in the coverage (reporters offering their personal opinions, speculations, or judgments without attributing them to any reporting) fell markedly, from 13 percent to 8 percent of the coverage. They were also less analytical in their reporting six weeks later. The amount of analysis reporting (interpretation attributed to some reporting) fell from 24 percent of the coverage to 18 percent.[3]

In time, however, the level of argument, speculation, interpretation, and judgment began rising again. A pattern seemed to emerge. When there was a fair amount of new information breaking at once, the press demonstrated skill in covering it, as with the impeachment proceedings in the House and Senate. But when the flow of information slowed, particularly in the aftermath of a big break in the story, the press seemed to try to fill the void with chatter and speculation. In the weeks after Lewinsky struck her immunity agreement with the independent counsel's office, for instance, the press seemed to become impatient as it waited for Starr's report to be delivered to Congress. In those five weeks, eight-month-old rumors speculating that Clinton had relations with still other women in the White House resurfaced in the press, as did gossip about what Starr's report might say about a cigar and other matters. During the Christmas break after the House impeachment of Clinton and before the Senate trial, old rumors about an illegitimate child Clinton had fathered with a black Arkansas prostitute resurfaced.

Why doesn't coverage of a story diminish when the flow of new information declines? Two reasons, we think, principally explain the phenomenon. The first is that so many news or information programs now exist with time to fill that there is a problem of excess capacity. Between 7 A.M. and midnight on a typical weekday in Washington, for instance, there are now 146 hours of news, information, and talk available to viewers on the local cable television system. A kind of Parkinson's Law comes into play here: the news expands to fill the time allotted—even if there isn't really enough news. (Increasingly, as we will discuss later, these channels also have not invested particularly in a reporting infrastructure, so they depend on inexpensive chat formats to fill the time.)

Second, when new information does break, there is a genuine surge in interest by the public to assimilate it. When the information flow slows, news organizations, trying to hold that audience, tend to overestimate how long the interest lasts and then tend to manufacture material to pass on. The effect is that of an aircraft carrier at full speed. Its sheer momentum propels it long after engines have been put to full stop.

In the end, how well did the press do? After the House Judiciary Committee finally took up the work of considering the evidence of the independent counsel, journalists had an unusual opportunity to assess the quality of their reporting in the form of the *Starr Report* and the more than three thousand pages of the supporting evidentiary material. The Committee of Concerned Journalists identified six story threads that went to the crux of the Clinton–Lewinsky case—whether the affair occurred and whether the president had obstructed justice and tampered with evidence to hide it.

The group then tracked the first appearance of each of these threads and its subsequent development in major news outlets in print, television, and the Internet, comparing what was reported to what was eventually contained in the *Starr Report* and evidentiary material. The goal was to make a disciplined and detailed examination of the coverage so as to balance accusations on both sides that the reporting had been proven substantiated or that it had been manipulated by misleading leaks.

The six threads were the existence of a blue dress with DNA evidence of the affair, the existence of witnesses of an affair, the existence of other staffers who had also had affairs with the president, the existence of talking points for Tripp and Lewinsky to lie about what they knew, the role of Vernon Jordan, and the role of Betty Currie.

We found, contrary to White House accusations, that those doing the bulk of the original reporting did not ferry false leaks and fabrications into coverage of the Clinton–Lewinsky story. At least in breaking stories initially, the press usually relied on legitimate sources and often was careful about the facts in the first account.

However, while the initial reporting of certain well-known stories such as the blue dress was proven right and none was made out of whole cloth, it is an oversimplification to say the press was vindicated.

Even in these careful stories, the press often tended to accept interpretations from sources uncritically and had a penchant to emphasize the perspective of investigators over those being investigated. In several important cases, the press leaned on suspicions of investigators that did not hold up. This was a factor in the coverage of Vernon Jordan, who (it was even reported at one point) had accepted a plea agreement with prosecutors, and of the so-called talking points, which some press reports falsely alleged that Clinton might have penned himself.

At other times, reporting was based on sources whose knowledge was secondhand, and this occasionally got journalists into trouble. This may have been the case in trying to report, without having heard the tapes, more subtle questions of law such as what Lewinsky told Tripp about Vernon Jordan. It also may have occurred in coverage of whether there was a third-party witness to an intimate encounter between the president and Lewinsky. The *Wall Street Journal* and the *Dallas Morning News* both ended up having to retract stories about possible third-party witnesses to encounters between Lewinsky and Clinton, in both cases, it later emerged, because their sources were second- or third-hand.

Others then used the reporting from elsewhere to engage in sometimes reckless speculation and propaganda. On occasion, the press also ferried speculation—some of which could have been construed as threats—from investigators into news accounts, raising questions about whether the press was sufficiently wary of being used by sources, especially law enforcement sources. This may have been the case, for example, in reporting on the so-called talking points Lewinsky gave Linda Tripp.

These tendencies to run with material call into question not only the fairness and accuracy of the coverage but also whether journalists in cases such as this stray into becoming in effect agents of the prosecution. In court papers, Starr himself, as we will discuss later, described his relationship with reporters as analogous to a relationship with informants.

Lastly, so much of the news media culture today involves commenting on the news rather than reporting it that in follow-up coverage, especially on television, the principle of keeping fact separate from suspicion and analysis separate from agenda-setting is no longer clearly honored. It was in the talk show arena that many of the rumors and unsubstantiated suspicions found their way into the mainstream media. The press itself has encouraged this by helping create a new class of activist pundits: loosely credentialed personalities who often thrive on being provocateurs. These people are treated as authorities, but they actually are neither news sources nor journalists. They lack the expertise to offer informal analysis. They also have no responsibility for impartiality or even accuracy. But the simple fact that they appear on these shows lends them and their assertions—whether solid facts or base rumor and innuendo—weight comparable to all other forms of journalism. Vague descriptions like "former prosecutor" or "senate aide" often mask their true function—TV personality. The argument culture may be undermining the reporting culture, and news organizations are helping encourage the process as they increase the range of programming and material they produce to chase a fragmenting audience.

Take a look at some of these story threads more closely.[4]

The Blue Dress: ABC was accurate in its first reporting that a stained dress of Lewinsky's would prove central to the Clinton–Lewinsky story. ABC's early reporting turned out to be highly accurate. The stain did turn out to be the president's semen. And although Lewinsky in her testimony maintained the dress wasn't, as ABC called it, "a kind of souvenir" (she said she thought the stain might have come from "spinach dip"), Linda Tripp's tapes of Lewinsky indicate otherwise.

ABC's initial report was based on a single source who, according to ABC, had "specific" knowledge of what Lewinsky had claimed.

Various factors may have led the media to later discount the story—its potential impact, its unsavory nature, the possibility that Lewinsky was lying, and the fact that ABC cited only a single source. On January 24, the *New York Times* incorrectly reported that the supposedly stained dress had been a gift from the president.

Other organizations picked up on the *Times*'s story, and when "the gift dress"—rather than the blue dress, which Lewinsky's mother was now holding—came back as "clean" from DNA testing, the media speculated, and the public assumed, that the stained dress story was wrong. The speculation spawned a series of reports on how the media had botched the coverage of the story in general, such as *Time* magazine's February 16 story "The Press and the Dress. The Anatomy of a Salacious Leak." This discounting was fueled by comments by William Ginsburg, Lewinsky's attorney, in which he dissembled about the dress enough to sound like a denial.

The attacks on the dress story, along with testimony leaks, made it easier for columnists and commentators to downplay the dress story after it reemerged. The attacks also made it more likely that the stories could be spun by the White House. One such comment: Geraldo Rivera's July 8 declaration, "[there is] absolutely no possibility that a so-called semen-stained dress exists," which was based on the fact that "Monica has insisted to everyone that things never went that far."

This confusion over the dress story points out an interesting argument. Was the reporting of the blue dress vindicated because it turned out to be accurate? Some journalists have argued no. It is not good enough that stories turn out to be correct, they argue. ABC was lucky, they contend, not good. The ends—whether a story is true—do not justify the means—a thin level of sourcing. That judgment may be too harsh. If ABC had good reason to believe its lone source—and it contends it did—that may be the result of having reliable sources, not luck.

The problem may be more subtle. Accuracy is certainly the first goal of journalism, but it is not the only one. Credibility and clarity are important as well. Before a news organization goes with a story, it needs to consider whether it has sourcing that is thorough enough that the account will be understood and believed. Making stories as clear and credible as possible, even if it means waiting, may also protect against stories' being mischaracterized in subsequent versions as they echo through the media.

The Talking Points: The day after the in Clinton–Lewinsky story broke, news organizations learned that on January 14 Monica Lewinsky had handed Linda Tripp a three-page document that began, "Points to make in an affidavit." The memo, which was dubbed the "talking points" in *Newsweek*'s America Online report, bedeviled news organizations for months though it scarcely makes an appearance in the *Starr Report*. At the height of the coverage, several different versions of the "official" memo emerged. In the January 22 online story, *Newsweek* reported that it was not clear who wrote the talking points, "but Starr believes that Lewinsky did not write them herself. He is investigating whether the instructions came from [Vernon] Jordan or other friends of the President." Because the memo was in pseudolegalese, it was assumed that Lewinsky did not write the talking points. In the coverage that followed the *Newsweek* report, many journalists accepted and repeated this line of thinking. The memo became a potential "smoking gun" (NBC, January 22, 1998; *USA Today*, July 1, 1998) that many news organizations were chasing and trying to link to various Clinton friends and confidants even after it was clear there were different versions of the memo. In its February 9 issue, *Time* magazine said, "Starr may have good reason to press [Bruce] Lindsey under oath."

On February 23, Fox News reported that Starr thought Clinton himself might have helped write the memo.

Talk show hosts and guests speculated about the authorship and the likelihood that the talking points represented witness tampering.

Fox News reported that it "has learned" that Lewinsky would not be immunized until she told who assisted in their writing.

After Lewinsky received immunity, several stories reported the talking points were no longer considered central to the investigation.

The *Starr Report* devotes just one paragraph and one footnote to the memo, saying that Lewinsky gave the document to Tripp and that she testified she wrote it herself perhaps with ideas from Tripp. The footnote says that in contrast Tripp testified she believed Lewinsky had assistance in drafting the talking points. The talking points are not mentioned among the "substantial and credible information that may constitute grounds for an impeachment."

The press cannot be held accountable for not knowing the authorship of the talking points. Nor is historical accuracy the standard by which the press should be accountable. Journalists can strive only for the best obtainable version of the truth at the time. But they can be held accountable for not reporting the limits of their knowledge and for not demonstrating a certain amount of skepticism for the information they gather.

Vernon Jordan: News organizations indicated almost immediately that Kenneth Starr was investigating Vernon Jordan for obstruction of justice. The reports said that Starr had tapes on which Monica Lewinsky said Jordan told her she should lie about her relationship with President Clinton. The initial January 21 *Washington Post* story, for instance, reported that Lewinsky told Tripp on tape of "Clinton and Jordan directing her to testify falsely."

ABC's *Good Morning America* reported the same day that sources said Lewinsky could be heard on a tape claiming the president told her to deny an affair and that Vernon Jordan "instructed her to lie."

The coverage in the following weeks included Jordan's denials, but tended to maintain that he might be in big trouble despite them. They sometimes characterized Jordan's statements as strategic or, as *Time* said in its February 2 issue, he was "wrapping himself in a protective layer of syntax."

The allegations against Jordan also spawned profiles that often depicted him as an amoral character, included pejorative anecdotes, and emphasized stories about his attitude toward women. A *Newsweek* profile in its February 2 issue, describing Jordan's relationship with Clinton, talked of how their "mutual fondness for the ladies is a frequent, if crude, topic of conversation"—a point repeated in other media accounts as well.

By February, particularly in talk show venues, Jordan was generally a suspect in the media accounts. *Meet the Press* aired a rumor, which ABC News later reacted to, that Jordan had been granted limited immunity by Starr, an assertion that implied Jordan was about to be charged with criminal conduct.

When Starr finally made his report to Congress, however, the case against Jordan was missing. Lewinsky admitted that, in fact, no one had told her to lie, and that she had told Jordan she did not have an affair with Clinton. The widely reported allegation that Lewinsky had said on tape that Jordan told her to just lie about it was wrong.

There is a prosecutors' memorandum that says Tripp asserted to investigators that "Jordan encouraged Lewinsky to lie." This may or may not have been available to the press at the time of their reporting but it is not supported by the evidence.

The closest Lewinsky comes on the tapes is the following:

> *Tripp:* But did he address the perjury issue at all? Because this is perjury.
> *Lewinsky:* OK he—Yeah. He said that—he said, "You are not gonna go to jail. You're not going to go to jail. *[and later]:* What he showed me is there's no way to get caught in perjury in a situation like this.

In her grand jury appearances, Lewinsky said she was lying when she said the above and that no one had told her to lie. Regardless, a careful reporter who heard this FBI tape would be reluctant to report that it makes a clear case for coaching the witness to lie. And a skeptical reporter might have decided the tape had an argumentative tone more than a conversational or narrative tone. If a reporter and an editor had heard this tape, one might have argued Tripp was pushing Lewinsky for answers and Lewinsky was obliging, but somewhat evasively.

The great majority of reporters, however, had not heard this tape, and should have been even more diligently skeptical about receiving investigative or prosecutorial leaks about it. In the *Starr Report* and supporting documents, the independent counsel does not suggest this tape reflects obstruction or witness-tampering. The *Starr Report* summarizes Vernon Jordan's testimony concerning his contacts with the president and his contacts with Monica Lewinsky, without any suggestion that he urged Lewinsky to lie or otherwise obstructed justice.

In the Jordan case, the media seemed eager to rush to judgment without having confirmation and to have used the allegations against

Jordan to pry into his personal life on topics that would normally be off limits and prejudicial.

Betty Currie: Shortly after the Clinton–Lewinsky story broke, Clinton's personal secretary, Betty Currie, was named as a potentially important link in Kenneth Starr's case—a key White House contact for Lewinsky. A round of personality profiles appeared that tried to put a face on the woman, which ranged from a motherly friend of Lewinsky to an adept keeper of presidential secrets.

The next set of stories, however, placed Currie in the eye of the media's coverage. On February 6, the *New York Times* reported Currie as telling investigators that Clinton had "called her into his office last month and led her through an account of his relationship" with Lewinsky that "differs in one critical aspect from her own recollections." The report added, "Currie had also retrieved and turned over to investigators several gifts . . . that the president had given Ms. Lewinsky," though "it is not clear who, if anyone, instructed Mrs. Currie to retrieve the gifts."

The *Times* piece was accurate and careful about details, both about the leading questioning and about the gift retrieval. A year later, the story holds up remarkably well even in small details. But it did place the response of Currie's lawyer, who said Currie knew of no ethical or legal violations, in the seventeenth paragraph.

Currie's lawyer gave a more detailed statement regarding the story, saying the account had been mischaracterized by a prosecutor's office leak. News organizations included the denial, but again tended to play up the angle, reflecting the prosecutors' belief, that Currie was working with the president to keep Lewinsky silent and that her testimony meant big trouble for the president.

Subsequent press accounts were far less careful than the one in the *New York Times*. The *Times*'s painstaking but suggestive wording of Clinton having "led" Currie through questioning, for instance, had become "being coached" on the NBC News *Today Show* that same morning. *Time* magazine would later say Clinton "tried to coach" Currie.

When Starr's report was released, it admitted that Clinton's discussions with Currie could have had other purposes—that he could have been "trying to refresh his memory" as Currie testified—but said it was much more likely that he was in fact coaching his secretary. In effect, this suspicion became the press's too.

On the question of the gifts, press accounts generally pointed out that it was not clear who ordered the gifts be returned, but they also implied that there was probably a less-than-innocent explanation. NPR's Nina Totenberg typified that tone on a broadcast of *Inside Washington:* "Betty Currie through her attorney has said the *New York Times* has mischaracterized her testimony. But you can't mischaracterize presents."

In the *Starr Report,* too, there is conflicting testimony over who called whom for the pickup of the gifts to take place, Lewinsky or Currie, or whether Clinton had instigated the exchange. Lewinsky said Currie called her. Currie said the opposite. The report concluded Lewinsky was more reliable.

Overall, the press performance here was mixed. The initial reporting based on anonymous sourcing was accurate in major details. This was not a case, as the White House alleged, of false leaks or disinformation. The press coverage, even the most speculative, seemed to capture the significance, legal and political, of both of the major allegations, the leading questioning by Clinton and the gift retrieval.

But some journalists declared that the allegations, if true, were proof of obstruction of justice, which may at least have been premature given the paucity of facts beyond what the *New York Times* was able to establish in its initial story. Regardless, the independent counsel's perspective, and that subsequently of the House Republicans, tended to be the prevailing tone of the media coverage.

Currie's side of the story, offered through her attorney, was downplayed.

Third Party Witnesses: From the earliest days of the story, reports were widely published both that there were third-party witnesses who had observed Clinton and Lewinsky in acts of intimacy, or, somewhat more cautiously, that Starr was reaching out to such potential eyewitnesses. Some subsequent reports included not-so-veiled warnings to Lewinsky that if she didn't agree to cooperate soon, Starr wouldn't need her much longer. Neither the *Starr Report* nor other supporting documents establish any eyewitnesses to acts of intimacy. Two serious problems are potentially raised here. One is that the press got ahead of the facts because it relied on secondhand sources. The other is that the press was being used by investigative or prosecutorial sources who wanted to employ the media to apply pressure on Lewinsky or other potential witnesses.

Several stories named potential eyewitnesses. On Sunday, January 25, ABC News reported, "the President and Lewinsky were caught in an intimate encounter in a private area of the White House.

It is not clear whether the witnesses were Secret Service agents or White House staff."

The following morning, both the *New York Post* and the *Daily News* led with the headline, "Caught in the Act" following the ABC report. Many other news organizations, including ABC, which was now changing its story, were reporting only that Starr was investigating allegations that there might be a third-party witness.

That evening, the *Dallas Morning News* moved a story on its Web site that it had prepared for the next day's paper, saying that a Secret Service agent would testify that he had seen Clinton and Lewinsky in a compromising situation.

The *Morning News* later that night would retract the story, but before it did, MSNBC, *Larry King,* and *Nightline,* among others, would carry the report and speculate on its consequences.

For the next week, speculation swirled about the witness or witnesses, with news organizations issuing and retracting reports. And in the months that followed the supposed witnesses surfaced and disappeared with little coming of predictions that the case was to be blown open.

On February 4, the *Wall Street Journal* reported on its Web site that White House steward Bayani Nelvis had testified before the grand jury that he had seen Clinton and Lewinsky together in the White House. The report had been posted online before its reporter had received a response from the White House to the allegation. *Wall Street Journal* Washington bureau chief Alan Murray then repeated the story on CNBC. The next day, however, the *Journal* changed its story in its print edition to say that Nelvis had not told the grand jury about the account, it had been Secret Service agents.

On February 9, the *Journal* retracted its story, reporting that Nelvis had told the grand jury that he had never seen Clinton alone with Lewinsky. In the evidentiary material, it would turn out, Nelvis had complained to Secret Service agents about having to clean up lipstick-stained towels, but he had never been an eyewitness. In addition, Secret Service agent Gary Byrne testified that another agent, John Muskett, told him of discovering Clinton and Lewinsky in a compromising moment. Muskett, however, denied it.

The case of the third-party witness story appears to raise several concerns.

One is whether the press was relying on secondhand sourcing in reporting about the alleged eyewitnesses. Journalists have acknowledged privately that at least some of the sources for some of these press accounts were not those directly involved in seeing the president and Lewinsky or even the investigators or prosecutors directly involved in the case. While a news organization may have two sources on a story, how much direct knowledge do those sources need to have before one can trust that a story has been verified? In this case, sources with direct first-hand knowledge would have knocked down these press stories and helped news organizations avoid embarrassment. Ironically, ABC to some extent escaped criticism because it never admitted to its error, even though it gave rise to several of the press accounts that followed.

Second, this also appears to be a case where investigators' and prosecutors' suspicions or suppositions made their way into the media coverage. The fact that these suppositions proved wrong raises questions about whether prosecutors' theories should be treated as news or should be handled with more restraint. It clearly appears that these investigative sources used the press to float rumors, to put pressure on potential witnesses including Lewinsky, and to try out a prosecution theory that included a possible conspiracy to cover up the affair. All this suggests that the press was not sufficiently skeptical in the case of the third-party witness thread about its sources and their motives.

A Second Intern: From early in the story, rumors circulated in Washington that one or more other women were about to be identified as involved with the president. For the most part, the rumors stayed at the level of cocktail party buzz, but some outlets in the Mixed Media Culture lean toward publication of such rumors, even by journalists who would not apparently do so in other venues.

On January 23—on *Rivera, Live!*—GOP pundit Ann Coulter stated as fact that Clinton had sex with "four other interns" in addition to Lewinsky. Two days later, Internet gossip columnist Matt Drudge appeared on NBC News's *Meet the Press* and was asked by anchor Tim Russert about reports that on the tape there are "discussions of other women, including other White House staffers, being involved with the president." Drudge replied, "There is talk all over this town. Another White House staffer is going to come out from behind the curtains this week. . . . There are hundreds, hundreds according to Ms. Lewinsky, quoting Clinton. . . ."

The allegation remained dormant in the media until August when Chris Matthews, hosting anti-Clinton publisher Lucianne Goldberg on his CNBC talk show *Hardball,* asked—in an invitation to float more rumors—whether there was another young intern involved with the president. "No, not an intern," Goldberg answered. "I know there were other women who were on staff who were involved. . . . These were women who were actively involved. It's all going to come out."

Two days later, journalist Fred Barnes of the *Weekly Standard* also floated the rumor on his Fox News program *The Beltway Boys*. "The Second Intern," he intoned. "Politicians, newspaper reporters, TV people, all around town, were talking about the possibility that there's a second intern who was sexually involved with the president. If there is, that will certainly be dynamite."

The second intern rumor quickly began to spread without documentation. The *New York Post* reported, "the Beltway is buzzing" that Bob Woodward of the *Washington Post* was "about to break a big exclusive about a second White House intern" and then included Woodward's response that this rumor was "absolutely untrue." Others followed until, a week later, the media reporter for the *Washington Post,* Howard Kurtz, did a story about the rumor, tracing its roots and showing that there was no substantial reporting behind the story. The rumor then dropped from publication.

The *Starr Report* has no reference to the rumors. Finally, while the press coverage did become more cautious as time passed, relying somewhat less on anonymous sourcing and punditry, the committee wanted to quantify the fact that this caution tended to be temporary. When the news slowed, the press tended to engage in periods of increased speculation. To track the anatomy of this caution followed by rumor-reporting, the study added a seventh story thread:

The Cigar: Washington summer gossip included a rumor that Lewinsky had used a cigar as a sex toy while with the president. It started with an Internet posting on the *Drudge Report,* was broadcast later the same day by Drudge on his Fox News Channel show, then spread to veiled references on the Sunday talk shows, then to the *London Times,* then to Jay Leno's monologue, then to a column in the *Washington Times* and elsewhere in the mainstream press as references to "kinky sex," including on *Meet the Press* and on one CNN talk program. In general, however, it is fair to say the press resisted spreading such rumors. The *Drudge Report* turned out to be wrong in some details, as did most of the reports flowing from it. But the *Starr Report* does include a sentence confirming a Clinton–Lewinsky use of a cigar in a sexual act.

In late August the rumor of Lewinsky using a cigar as a sexual toy began making the rounds in Washington. News organizations largely kept the salacious rumor out of the mainstream press. But the initial account on the *Drudge Report,* a sanitized version of which was broadcast by the Fox News Channel on Matt Drudge's show, did work its way cryptically into some reporting.

Perhaps on more than any other thread of the Clinton–Lewinsky story, this one was actually pushed forward by late night talk show monologues. Jay Leno, on August 24, made numerous references to the story. The story also found its way into newspapers through media columns that discussed how the media were handling the issue. On August 28, for instance, a Wesley Pruden column in the *Washington Times* had it both ways, writing about how newspapers, including his own, had avoided the details of "the President's cigar, the phallic toy, that Monica is said to have employed in the pantry, to the President's delighted applause."

The *Starr Report* differed in some key areas from the *Drudge Report.* Lewinsky testified to using the cigar sexually and to Clinton then putting it in his mouth and commenting on it.

But according to Lewinsky's testimony there was no mutual masturbation and the meeting was in general less sordid than the leaks.

There is also no support in the *Starr Report* for Drudge's allegation that Yasser Arafat was waiting in the Rose Garden when an encounter took place (the *Drudge Report* is not clear about what encounter it is writing about).

It is important to recall that in studies such as this it is not always possible to fully measure the press's caution, since the stories that were not aired because of diligence are impossible to credit. Mountains of accurate reporting about the background of the players on all sides, as well as corroborating evidence about Lewinsky's actions, about the Constitution, and the history of the White House, have all deepened the public's understanding and perceptions.

On the most basic level, however, the coverage of the Clinton–Lewinsky scandal demonstrates that the new Mixed Media Culture still relies for its initial breaking information largely on legitimate sources. Almost immediately, however, the Mixed Media Culture begins to push the story forward, even in the absence of new facts, and it is here that the weaknesses and tensions of the culture are exposed.

There is a growing tendency to follow stories up hastily by relying on thin or secondhand sources adding provocative new twists and what-ifs. This can involve ferrying speculation from sources who know some things but are only guessing about others. It also involves relying on prosecutors and accusers, who may be using the press to promote their agenda, threaten witnesses, or send up trial balloons. Whatever the case, follow-up stories today often include material that the originating news organization rejected as unsubstantiated when it was doing the more detailed initial reporting. This clearly occurred in the Betty Currie story. *New York Times* reporters and editors were careful to include only what they could verify from multiple sources. Within hours, material they had gathered but left out because they doubted its truth or found it impossible to prove was aired by competing news organizations that had done less reporting.[5]

Beyond the problem of follow-up reporting being thinner than the original work, there is a growing tension, as we will discuss later, between the press's role as gatherer of information and the press's role as merely a supplier of infotainment product. Much of the rush to judgment in this story, and in the new Mixed Media Culture, is a function of the press's relying on inexpensive chatter to fill space or air-time, or to appeal to an audience that wants emotions stirred rather than information.

The Clinton–Lewinsky story suggests that there is a growing problem of incompleteness in the Mixed Media Culture. Stories come out in piecemeal, an allegation now, followed by the counterallegation a few hours later. This not only makes tuning in inefficient, like looking at only one part of an elephant, it also creates a kind of numbness for the audience. In the continuous news cycle, the press never rests to sum up: here is what we know at the end of the day. It is forever pushing forward, grasping for the latest twist or dollop. Stories appear more confusing, more contradictory. Separating fact and allegation becomes more daunting.

This encourages sources, whether from those inside or close to the independent counsel's office or the White House, to manipulate the press. Haste and pressure to publish make the threshold verification easier to meet. And this is nowhere clearer than in the changing way that the press now deals with anonymous sources.

4

The Rise of Anonymous Sourcing

The second major finding of a close examination of the Lewinsky coverage and the New Media Culture concerns anonymous sourcing, both in the way the press described its sources and in the level of verification or the reliance on a single source.

In covering Watergate a quarter-century earlier, *Washington Post* executive editor Benjamin C. Bradlee established a rule for Bob Woodward and Carl Bernstein in their use of anonymous sources that became accepted as the industry norm and was thereafter deviated from only on occasion. Nothing could be used from an anonymous source unless it was confirmed by a second, independent anonymous source. In effect, the account of an anonymous source was treated as a tip until verified by additional reporting.[1]

By 1998, the two-source rule, if not dead, was no longer the rule. Nearly half (40 percent) of all reporting based on anonymous sourcing in the breaking days was based on a single anonymous source.

Only one statement in a hundred (1 percent of the reporting) was based on two or more named sources.

Just as significant as the enormous reliance on single anonymous sources was the remarkably vague manner in which the press described the anonymous sources it was relying on.

More than 83 percent of the time when relying on anonymous sources, the press failed to offer the public even the slightest hint of an anonymous source's possible allegiances or biases that might have affected the veracity of what the source was offering.[2]

Indeed, an examination of Clinton–Lewinsky coverage on selected days in January and March by the Committee of Concerned Journalists reveals that nearly half the time (43 percent), the press used only "source"—or "sources," the vaguest possible characterization—to describe anonymous sources.[3]

Another 16 percent of the time sources were characterized as merely being knowledgeable in a vague way, such as "sources familiar with the investigation" or "close to the investigation," a description that may establish some credibility but otherwise says little. Taken together, that means that six times out of ten (59 percent) the characterization of anonymous sourcing was essentially blind.[4]

And roughly one out of eight times (13 percent) the press described the job of the anonymous source, so that the public could at least assess on what basis the anonymous source might know the information they were imparting.[5]

Effectively, in other words, the methodology of the press in using anonymous sources was to tell the public, "a source told us this and we believe him and that's all we can tell you. Trust us to trust the source."

The characterization of anonymous sources varied greatly by media type. Print outlets went further in describing their anonymous sources' biases (23 percent of the time) and jobs (20 percent of the time) than did television outlets, which identified their sources' biases only 15 percent of the time and jobs only 5 percent of the time. And television outlets were much more likely to rely on the unattributed catchall phrase "we have learned" than print media, using it in 48 percent of all anonymous sourcing situations, while print media used it in only 1 percent of their anonymous source reporting.[6]

Was the Clinton–Lewinsky story unique? Did the press have to rely on a handful of largely blind sources because of the special circumstances in this case, in which a very few sources controlled nearly all the information? Or was this a sudden lowering of standards?

Perhaps it was neither. Listening to journalists from different generations react to the case, it becomes clear that there has been a structural change over time in the way the press deals with anonymous sources, and this change predated the Clinton–Lewinsky story.

Listen to this exchange at a February 1998 Committee of Concerned Journalists forum between Murray Marder, the retired diplomatic reporter for the *Washington Post*, and David Shribman, the *Boston Globe*'s Washington bureau chief, as the two discussed anonymous sourcing by several of the key journalists who covered the Lewinsky matter:[7]

> [T]he reporter can, in many ways which are not being used now in the press . . . indicate the direction the source comes from. . . . Is he coming from the right? Is he coming from the left? Is he coming from the Senate, from the Republicans in the Senate, from the Democrats in the Senate? I don't know what kind of deals you people make with sources, but when I dealt with sources all my life I don't allow them to say what I can't identify them with. All I'm giving them is anonymity for themselves, but I can still go ahead and say a White House source, a State Department source, a Capitol source. There are thousands of variations one can use. . . . I don't see why you can't go much further than you do in identifying the direction.
>
> Answered Shribman: "I think the identification of a source now is one of the opening parts of the negotiation in a journalistic conversation. I think from what you're saying, that that's a new development. But it surely is one of the opening. . . . In this context, the first thing you say is we agree, we have to agree on how you are to be described. That's a negotiating point. And not really different from the kind of negotiations, in a way, that Ken Starr goes through when he's deciding whether to offer immunity.
>
> Marder: Is that really the way you start your conversation? It's certainly not the way they've been started for the last 50 years that I know of.
>
> Shribman: I think increasingly that's the case.

Early academic research appears to reinforce that the shift toward a reliance on trusting anonymous sources to make allegations, with a limited amount of independent verification by the press, is a trend long in building. Increasingly, says Tom Patterson of the Shorenstein Center at Harvard, "Allegations that surface in the news based on claims by sources are not combined with factual digging on the reporters' part. . . . That tendency increased in the 1980s, increased again in the 1990s."[8]

Several researchers are finding a similar trend, even in journalism overseas.[9]

Is there anything wrong with this growing reliance on anonymous sources? On one level knowing the identity of a source is irrelevant. The point of reporting is enlightening the public. As long as a reporter is confident about the information he is getting, does it really matter where it is coming from?

William Kristol, the editor of the *Weekly Standard,* argues that when he served as former Vice President Dan Quayle's chief of staff, the *Washington Post*'s White House reporter, Ann Devroy, relied heavily on background information and quotes. And Devroy's approach, he maintained, had gotten "much more information out of the White House than other reporters."[10]

Kristol is right. Offering anonymity sometimes can be the only way to gain access to certain sources, or to a level of candor from those sources, because it protects the sources from retribution for their cooperation. Carl Bernstein contends, "[In Watergate] I don't think we ever named a source. Because it would have been impossible to pursue the story without the use of anonymous sources."[11] The amount of anonymous sourcing on the Clinton–Lewinsky story, roughly 40 percent of all news gathering in the first week, may not be surprising, given the limited number of sources who actually had knowledge on this story.

A source who is anonymous is a source who is less accountable for his or her words. That may allow the source to be more candid to the journalist, without facing consequences. The lack of accountability, however, can work the other way, too. The source now can mislead, misdirect, control the interpretation of events, or decide how much information is provided with a greater degree of impunity. The source is not only less accountable for telling the truth, in other words, but is less accountable for lying or misleading as well. The source has, in effect, usurped the editor's role in determining how the news will be presented.

A second key issue in evaluating the veracity of anonymous sources involves how many sources are required. Given the selectivity and subjectivity of memory, it might be considered a law of human nature that two sources are always better than one, three better than two, and so on. This holds regardless of whether the sources are named or not. There are cases certainly where a single anonymous source may be impeccable, if he or she is a principal and the reporter knows the information is dead on. When the *Washington Post* in March reported on Clinton's testimony during his deposition in the Paula Jones case, the paper clearly had a full transcript of the deposition or perhaps even a videotape (since it described his expressions as well as his words). Although the paper did not describe what it had or how it had acquired it, the account was never assailed from any side.

But realistically, such a single source is a rare case. More often, far more often, more sources are better than fewer.

Assuming the journalist is satisfied with a source's honesty, how much description must the journalist share with the audience? Should the journalist share with the audience some of his or her rationale for trusting the source, such as saying it is a source who has proven reliable in the past? How does the audience assess the accuracy of information? Is it enough for a citizen to say, "Well, I trust ABC News. If it's good enough for them, it's good enough for me"?

ABC's Jackie Judd, her network's lead reporter on the story, says she had thought hard about the issue of sourcing as Clinton–Lewinsky developed and decided she was giving viewers the information they needed. "One day when I was sitting at my computer struggling with this, how do I define a source in this story? I said, well, knowledgeable. Of course they're knowledgeable. Why else would I be including them in the story? That doesn't help a viewer.

"I think . . . there's nothing inherently awful with just saying 'a source.' Usually in the context of the report you can guess which side the person is coming from."[12]

It is useful to take a moment here to explore what offering anonymity implies. If a basic principle of journalism is transparency, full disclosure, then granting a source anonymity is by definition an exchange in which the journalist is giving up an important principle. The complex test is how much disclosure the journalist is giving up and what level of candor or special access he or she is gaining in exchange.

That trade should not be taken lightly. Journalists should weigh carefully how much they are giving away. What is often forgotten is that in the case of anonymous sources, specificity and precision can make all the difference in determining what information actually means.

Consider for instance, this statement: "Many inside the White House believe the president committed adultery."

Are those "many" two twenty-something staffers in the Old Executive Office Building, who have no direct knowledge? Do they include the first lady and her chief of staff?

Or consider this statement: "Those familiar with the investigation now believe that Kenneth Starr has the evidence necessary to indict the president for perjury."

If the source is identified as "an attorney close to Paula Jones" it may mean any number of things, from the truth to wishful thinking. If the source is "an attorney on Ken Starr's staff" it may mean something else—perhaps that the aide wants to push Starr to indict, or perhaps that it will happen, or perhaps that it was floated to put pressure on a potential witness.

If the identity of the source can alter not only the reliability of an allegation but even its possible meanings or implications, then clearly more disclosure in characterizing anonymous sources becomes a matter of high importance to the consumer of the news. Although television places a premium on leaving out all but the most essential narrative, in the case of describing anonymous sources we believe Judd is mistaken. This information is vital.

There is another problem with minimal description of a source, which might be called the dissemination factor. Whatever identification a journalist gives a source in the original account is certain to diminish as the story makes its way through the merged media echo chamber, from the AP recap to the thirty-second "tell story" on the local news, down to the radio news headline and the angry reaction on a talk show. In many cases news organizations are held to account by the public for how their stories are treated elsewhere. It is increasingly important for journalists to anticipate these consequences of dissemination and try to write their stories in ways that make their original context clear.

ABC's Judd admitted suffering the ravages of the echo chamber in the case of a piece she did about Kathleen Willey, another woman who had alleged President Clinton had pursued her sexually. Judd's story reported that Willey was claiming she had been pressured to deny that Clinton had groped her. Specifically, Willey was claiming that a Democratic fundraiser named Nathan Landow had pressured her. Judd's story was full of careful nuancing. She wasn't reporting that Landow had done this, only that Willey was claiming it. In fact Judd reported that Landow denied it.

But her delicate qualifiers disappeared as the story was retold. "What happened with what we thought was a well-reported piece was, it shows up in other media as 'ABC News has reported that Nate Landow pressured Kathleen Willey not to tell about this alleged advance by the President.' That is not what we reported."[13]

If journalists anticipate the echo effect, they could make the limits of what they know and report clearer. Judd, for instance, might state explicitly what this story is *not* saying, as a way of warning others away from misinterpreting it. The echo effect makes the need for precision greater than ever before.

The most important question, in the end, is, how can journalists tell the truth from a lie? One answer is that this is what journalists are paid to do. It might be considered the professional instinct model, often called "a bullshit detector." If gut feelings were adequate, however, why was there a two-source rule in the first place? The argument for journalistic instinct implies that journalists have some kind of common training or that over time they develop an ability to see through deception. Accordingly, there would evolve a kind of marketplace of truth, in which the work of the sloppiest journalist is drowned out by the work of the best, in which errant information is quickly corrected by more accurate, perhaps even in which there is a penalty for being wrong. Unfortunately, while it is sometimes true—reporting by other news outlets quickly helped raise doubts about CNN's flawed report repeated in *Time* magazine of the use of nerve gas in Vietnam—it is clearly not always the case that accuracy prevails. The Clinton–Lewinsky story showed how live reporting of unverified information often moves faster than that which is verified. In the current climate, spectacular simplification easily overwhelms the dull and complex truth.

News organizations may even be penalized more for admitting their mistakes at times. The *Boston Globe,* for instance, became the object of high controversy when its own in-house policing blew the whistle on one of its columnists, Patricia Smith, for making things up. The *Globe*'s high standards then forced it to examine another popular columnist, Mike Barnicle. Months of public and internal agonizing followed, until Barnicle was eventually forced to resign. The paper's desire to have and make clear its standards, in other words, came at great public and internal cost, at least in the short run. Standards are also difficult to manage and oversee, the *Globe* case revealed. *Globe* editors and its publisher suffered through a lengthy period of criticism because of their good intentions. In a similar manner, the *Dallas Morning News* is remembered in the Clinton–Lewinsky saga as the paper that fumbled the third-party witness story, largely because it had the courage and honesty to retract its story when one of its sources got cold feet, a source that turned out to have only indirect knowledge. Other news organizations, such as ABC News, had similar reports of a third-party witness that to this day remain unsubstantiated. But they have escaped some of the criticism because they have never admitted the story was wrong.

As painful as they can be and as difficult as they are to manage, high standards serve a larger purpose that makes the negative publicity they may bring worthwhile. Standards that are enforced publicly make reporters and editors more careful and more skeptical of the information they receive. They create an incentive for accuracy, rather than just for exciting copy. They raise the stakes of failure.

Journalists who believe they can simply tell when a source is offering the full truth, based on professional experience and instinct, are probably fooling themselves. In the case of a fast-moving national story, journalists would be better served by developing some concrete protocols within their individual newsrooms to evaluate a source's reliability.

A few journalists have. *New York Times* executive editor Joseph Lelyveld, for instance, describes two questions that he believes his reporters and editors should ask themselves before using an anonymous source:

- How much direct knowledge does the anonymous source have of the event?

- What if any motive might the source have for misleading us, gilding the lily, or hiding important facts that might alter our impression of the information?

Only if they are satisfied by the answers will they use the source. This test protected the *New York Times* on multiple occasions in covering the Clinton–Lewinsky saga.

Deborah Howell, the Washington editor and bureau chief of Newhouse Newspapers, also has a set of protocols about when and how she will use anonymous sources:

- She will use them only to provide information that can be independently verified unless the source has unique direct knowledge.

- She won't use anonymous sources to render opinions.

- She won't allow her reporters to lead a story with a blind quote.

Lelyveld's test helps sort out whether to believe an anonymous source. Howell's test guides how to use them. They complement each other.

We suggest they can both be strengthened by adding two more rules.

The first augments Lelyveld's test of believability. We think a journalist should ask him or herself:

- How well does the journalist know the source? In other words, has the journalist relied on this source in an investigative and anonymous context before? If so, has the source ever misled the journalist?

If you add this question of personal history to the question of the source's knowledge and motives, it covers much of the ground one might have for deciding whether to trust a source.

If one then applied Howell's rule of using only what can be and has been verified with other sources, you may have reached the highest level of subjective testing you can give.

Yet even on top of that, we suggest one other additional concept to raise the level of accuracy. Implicit in the bargain is that the source is telling the truth.

- If it turns out the source is lying, journalists should make it clear that any anonymity agreement is voided. In other words, the anonymity protection does not extend to cases of deliberate disinformation. If the news organization establishes a penalty for lying, it can help reset the balance, somewhat, between sources and journalists in the context of anonymous sourcing.

Journalists, however, must be careful. There is a difference between disinformation and misinformation. As Clinton's impeachment trial was winding down in the Senate, English journalist Christopher Hitchens involved himself in the story by telling friends that White House aide Sidney Blumenthal had misled prosecutors. Blumenthal had denied in his sworn testimony to House impeachment managers that he was the source of erroneous stories characterizing Lewinsky as a stalker of the president. Hitchens announced that over lunch one day Blumenthal had passed along that allegation about Lewinsky, though Hitchins himself had never turned around and published the allegation. Was Hitchens right in outing Blumenthal this way? The case is difficult for two reasons.

First, Hitchens and Blumenthal were personal friends, and it was not at all clear that Blumenthal was acting as a source in this case. "We knew each other too well to have, so to speak, groundrules," Hitchens said of the encounter. What's more, even Hitchens didn't believe Blumenthal intended to plant a story with him. "He [Blumenthal] has known since at least 1992 that I have nothing but contempt for President Clinton. So I don't think that he can possibly have expected that I would do him this favor" [of publishing the rumor that Lewinsky had stalked the president].

Second, it is not clear that Blumenthal was deliberately lying if he did pass on this rumor. If he repeated only what the president had told him and was clear about the limits of what he knew, then Blumenthal would have been telling reporters the truth as far as he knew it.

If journalists are to employ an anonymous sourcing contract, first they must make the contract known to the interviewee—it works as much as a preventive measure as punitive one. Second, journalists probably should set the bar at disinformation. Any source can be mistaken. If a journalist errs by publishing information a source knew only secondhand, it is the journalist who is at fault, not the source.

Some might suspect that exposing sources who lie wouldn't work in practice because journalists would worry that other sources might get cold feet. In fact, it has happened. Actually, this has been a rule at the *New York Times* since the 1960s. A handful of other news organizations have instructed sources in this manner. The rule may not always be universally observed or even fully made clear to reporters. It should be. The so-called contract of anonymity becomes merely a way in which sources manipulate journalists if it is a one-sided bargain. It must contain risk for the source who abuses it.

If the tests we suggest here for anonymous sources seem subjective, having some method at least implies that the journalist is seeking truth, not just looking for an excuse to go with the story. Establishing even that much with the public is a step in the right direction toward reaffirming credibility.

5

The Growing Power of Sources

If anonymous sourcing is not so benign, why has there been such a move toward relying on it?

One reason is that increasingly the public statements that are on the record seem so contrived. Marlin Fitzwater, the presidential spokesman for Presidents Reagan and Bush, says sources have begun to use "on-the-record" to spin in ways that have evolved far beyond what he saw during the late 1980s and early 1990s. And it is not restricted to skilled politicians. In the post-O.J. era, lawyers, a group that not long ago eschewed the media, now rush to the cameras to "set the stage" for their clients with the public. "The cameras are waiting for them when they emerge from the courthouse. . . . A lawyer walks out and says whatever is most advantageous to his client . . . [with] no allegiance to the truth in that situation. . . . [H]e has totally usurped any editing prerogatives of the press by utilizing that on-the-record and on-camera situation. His words then become a part of the lexicon, a part of the understanding of the problem, right or wrong."[1]

This was refined to a new art in the O.J. case, Fitzwater suggested. "Now we see it in every case that comes up."

In Watergate, Carl Bernstein recalls that he and Bob Woodward were interviewing the principals in the story multiple times, even those testifying to the grand jury. In this case, every major source was quickly "lawyered up." Until the Senate trial ended, Monica Lewinsky never spoke publicly; nor did Linda Tripp. Meanwhile Lewinsky's attorney, William Ginsburg, became for a time a media omnipresence. Interestingly, when Lewinsky's legal needs changed and she decided to cut a deal, she hired new attorneys. The new guys, Plato Cacheris and Jacob Stein, were Washington veterans whose approach more closely followed the city's time-tested modus operandi, that of behind-the-scenes dealers. The difference between the stonewalling, highly public approach of Ginsburg and the quiet and more anonymous legal maneuvering of Cacheris-Stein suggests that managing the press outside the courtroom and handling someone's needs inside the grand jury room are two different things.

The architecture of television is a factor here. In the mixed media age of the twenty-four-hour news cycle, the first impression the public gets is increasingly unedited and live. There is little opportunity for the reporter to leaven the lawyer's remarks by other reporting, or to juxtapose this lawyer's account with the opposing view. That will come at the next competing live event.

Often journalists are used as props in these situations, as was demonstrated with one of the more curious press conferences in the Clinton–Lewinsky saga. On the second day of the story, Independent Counsel Kenneth Starr announced he was going to have a press conference. The media arranged itself in its usual tableau around the news maker—an uncontrolled mob, jostling and shouting, armed with microphones, wires, and Ikagami cameras. That gave Starr the opportunity to pretend that he was shocked by the response, that there had been some mistake, and that his appearance would be just a photo opportunity. The result was a picture on the network news that evening of Starr looking besieged by the press—rather than Starr besieging the president, as his Democratic party critics were alleging of him.

Even some champions of press freedom have begun to figure this out. Roone Arledge of ABC acknowledged that increasingly the press leave the impression of besiegers in these photo opportunities, attacking those who make the news, an image "we should be ashamed of."

"Most of the kinds of pictures [we get when] we victimize these poor people are not exclusive. They are not journalism. They are photo ops," Arledge said.[2]

Arledge suggested that the press form voluntary pools for these gang bangs "to which everyone is invited. . . . Ultimately, with digital cameras, there is no reason why still photographers cannot do the same thing—and let us go out and have two cameras instead of two hundred."

Arledge's suggestion has yet to be adopted. The intense competition and sense of individuality bred into news organizations makes such cooperation difficult. News organizations tend to collaborate on such ideas as pools—even when such agreements serve their self-interest—only when they are imposed by news makers at the White House or Pentagon as a condition of getting access. The general explanation is that journalists reflexively resist anything that might inhibit their ability to differentiate themselves from rivals, even when that differentiating really means nothing. Unfortunately, however, they tend to resist collaboration even when their resistance has the effect of granting more leverage to those who would manipulate them.

The result leads to poorer journalism and a public less well served. In an atmosphere when public statements appear so contrived that even the journalists consider them little more than pseudonews, for instance, anonymity takes on a new meaning. The quote that appears somehow covert can seem more authentic and therefore more reliable. If it is secret, if we are privy to something "revealed," it must be more important—and maybe more honest.

The paradoxical perception that the anonymous quote is somehow the more genuine, however, is often an illusion that merely reflects the fact that the press has less and less access.

The growing leverage over the press by those who make news is not only a reflection of their growing sophistication. It is also a function of simple mathematics.

With more outlets for news, the authority of any one of those outlets to set the terms of the discussion with a source is diminished. Journalists know that even if they or their direct competitors might not agree to the terms of a source, some other outlet in a different point on the media spectrum will—be it Matt Drudge or G. Gordon Liddy. In either case, the mainstream journalist may be chasing soon enough.

The two trends have given sources what some observers see as a new arrogance. As we learn more about how the Clinton White House operates, Fitzwater, said: "You see a picture of the White House that I don't recognize. You see a White House that intimidates, that attacks the press, that threatens them with putting them out of business and never talking to them and never giving interviews and withholding stories. And you see a media reacting to it, allowing themselves in many cases to be intimidated in ways I never really thought was possible."[3]

Fitzwater may be right about intimidation, but the practice began well before Clinton's White House tenure. Fitzwater's predecessor, Reagan White House spokesman Larry Speakes, employed similar bullying tactics. He would denounce reporters who had criticized or challenged him and threaten to put them "out of business," which meant he would no longer answer the phone calls or talk to them. He would even do this in public to intimidate other reporters. NBC News correspondent Chris Wallace was frozen out for years. Fitzwater himself, while he didn't employ intimidation, was hardly unsophisticated in the Bush and Reagan White Houses in the art of massaging and manipulating the press. Like Mike McCurry, he was far more genial about it.

Today, however, many other sources increasingly believe they can manipulate the press—or even mislead it—with growing impunity. Lucianne Goldberg, the New York publishing executive, goes so far as to claim to have controlled the Clinton–Lewinsky story. Her son describes it as "a Goldberg conspiracy."[4] It may be a perverse form of self-aggrandizement on the Goldberg family's part, but certain basic facts are clear. Goldberg used ongoing discussions with *Newsweek* correspondent Isikoff to find out what threshold level of proof the press would need to publish the story. She and Linda Tripp then helped manufacture that evidence by directing the nature of the conversations between Tripp and Lewinsky and directing Tripp to tape them. She and Tripp then gave the story an official investigative patina so important to the press by contacting Starr's office and offering him the tapes, in part, because they knew that they still had not succeeded in persuading *Newsweek* to run with it. They provided *Newsweek* with the tapes that helped verify the authenticity of the story—*Newsweek* did not ask for them. And Tripp then cooperated with Paula Jones's attorneys on the eve of Clinton's deposition that Saturday so that they could ask Clinton about the Lewinsky relationship based on the tapes that created the basis for Starr's ultimate case, that Clinton lied about the Lewinsky relationship in the Jones deposition. When *Newsweek* didn't break the story, Goldberg was considered the main suspect for leaking it to Matt Drudge.[5]

If Goldberg's arrogance toward the press stems from the idea that she knows how to control it, others feel they can operate freely because the news media are something that can now safely be ignored. One U.S. senator, speaking only on background, described his attitude about journalism today this way. When he decided to move up from the House to the Senate, he went to the retiring senator in his state for counsel about how to deal with the media in their state. "Ignore them," he recounted the retiring senator as saying. "They only make mischief, but increasingly they're irrelevant. TV doesn't cover politics locally, so ignore it. Only half the people in our state get a newspaper. Only half who get it read it. Only half who read it remember it. Only half who remember believe it. You can consider the press irrelevant."

"I did," the senator said. "And I won."[6]

He did so with a blitzkrieg of negative advertising that was widely assailed in the press. Yet the senator is now one of the key political strategists in his party. "He is the new paradigm," said one political consultant who is familiar with the senator and influential in party circles.

Massachusetts Representative Barney Frank, one of the more adept at using the press, goes even further. He believes that not only is press attention often overrated, but for a politician with a safe seat anonymity may be safer politically. "Unless you're planning to run for president, which for a number of reasons I'm not, attention is not all that important. In fact inattention is better, and in a good year it may be filing deadline before they know you're up again."[7] Indeed, Frank contends, inattention may also serve the public interest as well as a politician's personal interest. The press's exaggerated fascination with conflict can hinder the necessary process of finding common ground and compromise in negotiations over legislation, he argued. The best press of his life came when he became a florid critic of Speaker Newt Gingrich, not for the compromises he made in earlier years to pass legislation. "I remember Frank Bellotti, former attorney general of Massachusetts, telling a group of us about twenty years ago, then young state legislators as we were looking for our names in a newspaper story, 'You'll know you're serious about this business when you pick up the paper hoping the Christ your name isn't in it.'"[8]

Still other politicians believe that the press is increasingly something to be manipulated more than feared. A top-ranking political consultant working with one of the presidential aspirants in the year 2000 said privately, "There is definitely a greater sense that politicians and those who work for them can say what we want, mislead or even worse, and be less likely to be punished for it."[9] Why?

"Because," she continued, "we know how to play your game, how to document what we say, even if it is arguable, and because you have less a sway over the public anyway."

Indeed, a declining audience for the press is one reason politicians feel this way. Declining trust in the press is another reason. As the public believes journalists less, the press's ability to play watchdog over the veracity of the political debate is naturally diminished.

Again, it is important to make clear that anonymous sourcing is a critical part of the journalist's tool box, particularly for the watchdog journalist. It is sometimes the only way to protect the whistle blower or woo cooperation from a reluctant but honest source. That is why, indeed, we cannot identify the sources of the quotations just given. Yet journalists need to recognize that its increased use is not necessarily a sign of their leveraging more information on behalf of the public. Journalists may be resorting to background sourcing more because they are in a weaker position, which makes anonymity more dangerous, not more useful.

In short, the press should be exercising more caution about anonymity today. Instead, it is exhibiting less. The danger of this is highlighted in part by a peculiar sidelight of the Clinton–Lewinsky saga, the relations between Independent Counsel Kenneth Starr and the press.

If the coverage of the scandal at certain points showed a penchant to reflect the suspicions of prosecutors and investigators out of balance with the denials of the accused, this would hardly be unusual, whether the case be Richard Jewell or countless other accused citizens whose cases are covered in the press. It does, however, reflect a growing tendency of media coverage.

A generation ago, it was not uncommon for news organizations to have policies against naming the accused in cases until charges were filed. Those policies are largely gone now, and while they may never have applied to politicians, the changing of these standards reinforces the importance of a press skeptical of being used by investigative arms of the government.

In Clinton–Lewinsky, the issue may be particularly important given the stakes involved. It may also be important because Starr himself in trying not to disclose his contacts with the press has alluded to his relationship with reporters as being analogous to a relationship with informants.

Starr has been accused of leaking prejudicial grand jury material in an attempt to shape opinion in the Lewinsky case. (His accusers include opposing counsel and an array of editorial writers, columnists, and commentators including Anthony Lewis, Albert R. Hunt, Lars-Erik Nelson, and Steven Brill.)

The judge in charge of the Starr grand jury gave credence to those accusations by ordering Starr to show cause why he should not be held in contempt of court for leaks. The judge's order does not confirm prosecutorial misconduct, but places the burden on Starr to disprove the charge that he violated the federal Rules of Criminal Procedure by improperly divulging grand jury secrets. Judge Norma Holloway Johnson wrote: "The Court finds that the serious and repetitive nature of disclosures to the media of Rule 6(e) material strongly militates in favor of conducting a show cause hearing."

Starr sought to stay a hearing on the subject by arguing that his anonymous dealings with reporters should be treated the same as an investigator's dealings with confidential informants.[10]

Some reporters found troubling the suggestion that Starr was using journalists as informants, but his argument to that effect got little attention in the press. The court was hearing arguments on the leaks in closed session. Heavily redacted transcripts were then released weeks or months later, if at all. Major news organizations went to court in an attempt to force these proceedings out in the open.[11]

In the fall of 1998, the Committee of Concerned Journalists sent questionnaires to more than 270 journalists around the country, asking them about the practice of trading information from their reporting with law enforcement officials in return for more information. Interestingly, the practice is far less accepted than many in Washington might have thought. Overall, 60 percent of journalists surveyed disapproved of the practice. Thirty-five percent saw it as acceptable. Another 4 percent considered it acceptable on rare occasions.[12]

In addition, a large percentage of the respondents felt compelled to write explanatory comments, far more than on any other question in the survey. Those explanations fell into five categories.

Of those who thought it was acceptable, even the most lenient acknowledged some risk.

- That it was acceptable but could be risky.

- It was acceptable only if you receive more information than you give away.

- It was acceptable only if you were providing public or previously published information.

Of the 60 percent majority that disapproved of bartering with law enforcement sources for information, there were two distinct camps of comments.

- This was not an acceptable practice because journalists are not an arm of the law and lose their trustworthiness and objectivity if they do this.

- This was not an acceptable practice except in those unusual circumstances where the information traded was in a clear public service, such as helping solve a crime, identifying a witness, or saving a life, but not as a tit-for-tat barter.

The story of who was leaking to the press and why received little notice in the mainstream media because news organizations had invested time and resources to establish a relationship with the Office of Independent Counsel.[13] It is also difficult for news organizations to cover a story in which they are actors, and in this case it may even have hindered their relations with Starr. In the end, however, the story might be best analogized to the elephant at a dinner party: if nobody paid attention, maybe it would go away.[14]

6

There Are No Gatekeepers Here

If the Clinton–Lewinsky story illustrated the rising leverage of those who want to make news as well as those who want to manipulate it, it also demonstrated a third trend transforming the press culture: The proliferation of news outlets and the development of shorter news cycles have left news organizations increasingly unable to maintain or even define their own ethical standards.

Information is moving so fast, news outlets are caught between trying to gather new information and playing catch-up with what others have delivered ahead of them. The result for any news organization is a set of flexible standards that are often bent beyond recognition as the organization relies on another's reportage.

There were scores of examples in the Lewinsky case. In the first week alone, 12 percent of all reports were attributed to other news organizations and unverified by the news outlet recounting them. If you count only the reporting of facts—and eliminate the analysis and opinion offered in that first week—the percentage of unverified secondhand reporting is closer to 20 percent of all reporting.

It is too easy to simply wring hands and point fingers. How to cope with unverified facts and rumors today is one of the most complex aspects of contemporary journalism. To fully understand how difficult it can be, it would be helpful to consider two examples.

The first is the case of the notorious semen-stained dress.

Within days of the Lewinsky story's breaking, at least one source familiar with the Lewinsky–Tripp tapes was telling reporters all over Washington that the intern claimed to have a blue dress stained with semen as a memento. As the dress allegation circulated, reporters puzzled over what to do with it.

The rules of when a story is verified are so varied that even so-called mainstream news organizations viewed the dress allegation quite differently.

The *Los Angeles Times* almost ran with it and then eventually decided the evidence was "insufficient," as Washington bureau chief Doyle McManus put it. Why? Its reporters had not actually heard the tapes. Moreover, even if Lewinsky claimed to have the dress, was she telling the truth? (There were already reports in circulation, including Lewinsky's own descriptions of herself on tape, that she was not a completely honest person.)

The story raised an interesting subtlety: does a news organization have to be more sure of a story's truth depending on the seriousness of the allegation? If a news organization wants to suggest there is DNA evidence proving the president committed a crime—in this case lying under oath in denying a sexual relationship with Lewinsky—should it be more certain of its accuracy than in describing the president's mood in a policy meeting? Do the rules of journalism change with the stakes of the story? McManus's caution was greater because the story was potentially so explosive.

ABC News arrived at a different determination from that of the *Los Angeles Times.* Reporter Jackie Judd initially planned to leave the dress out of her report. "I thought," she described later, "oh, this is just too much over the line. We're talking about the president of the United States here. But I think my editors rightly pointed out that if what Monica Lewinsky said was true, it would represent forensic evidence which would go to the legal issues, the core of what the story is really about."[1]

At ABC, in other words, the seriousness of the allegation made it more important to use it.

The day after the ABC account, Lewinsky attorney William Ginsburg was then asked about the dress at a press conference and denied its existence. With that, the *Los Angeles Times* felt compelled to then use the dress allegation it had earlier left out, or at least reference it well down in its account of Ginsburg's remarks. "There had been speculation that semen on Lewinsky's clothing could be used to establish a DNA link to Clinton. Ginsburg said he had no knowledge of any stained dress."[2]

Or consider the case of *Newsweek* and the blue dress.

Newsweek kept it out of its first account, and Isikoff refused to even comment on the allegation when pressed about it in the loosest possible way by Matt Lauer of the *Today Show*. Lauer was acting on a comment from Matt Drudge, whom Lauer had interviewed earlier that morning.

> *Lauer:* I'd like your reaction to something Matt Drudge just said about a possible DNA trail. . . .
> *Isikoff:* Matt, look, there's a lot of things I've heard about this and other things. I—I . . .
> *Lauer:* Have you heard that, though?
> *Isikoff:* I have not reported that, and I'm not going to report that until I have evidence that it is, in fact, true.
> *Lauer:* You're not telling me whether you've ever heard it?

Four days later, *Newsweek* did run with it, though it still had not talked to Lewinsky or developed any physical evidence that such a dress existed. Nor had Isikoff or anyone at *Newsweek* heard the tapes. Why? ABC had now run with the story.

The case of the third-party witness to an intimate encounter between Clinton and Lewinsky offered another example of the press being uncertain of standards.

After ABC broke the accusation, citing unnamed sources on ABC's *This Week* program, the press moved in varying directions. The *New York Post* and *New York Daily News* both put it on their covers under the headline "CAUGHT IN THE ACT." The source they cited: ABC News.

The *New York Times* came close to publishing an article about the accusation, then decided at the last minute not to do so. On early Sunday, the paper had four sources backing the account of an interrupted intimate encounter, but as the day wore on, the sources fell by the wayside. By 6 P.M. the paper killed the story, after deciding the sources had all gotten their information secondhand from the same source.[3] "We worked very hard on this story and in the end we weren't sure what was true," said Joseph Lelyveld, the executive editor.[4]

The *Chicago Tribune* took a different course. It wasn't sure either, but decided to use the allegation and let readers know it had no idea of its reliability. It put the accusation in the second paragraph of its lead article on the case, also citing ABC News. The third paragraph began with the caveat, "if true," and acknowledged that "attempts to confirm the report independently were unsuccessful."[5]

The issue implicit in the blue dress and third-party witness stories is an important one.

The classic definition of the journalist's role by Walter Lippmann is to sift out rumor and innuendo from fact and publish what one believes are facts.[6]

Wrote Lippmann: "The news of the day as it reaches the newspaper office is an incredible medley of fact, propaganda, rumor, suspicion, clues, hopes, and fears, and the task of selecting and ordering that news is one of the truly sacred and priestly offices in a democracy."

The question today is whether the old definition still holds. Can the press still aspire to be in the truth business, to say, in effect, "if you read it here, you can believe it?" Or are there so many outlets now—is information such a commodity—that the press can no longer play gatekeeper to verifiable facts; instead, its job is to survey everything the public has heard from the cacophony of sources and help people sort through it?

Ted Koppel believes that in today's intensely competitive media environment there is more pressure than ever to run with a story that may not be solidly verified. The competition, particularly that created by twenty-four-hour news networks, "lends itself to people putting material on the air before they have gone through the discipline of reporting," Koppel said. "And it is, when it's properly done, it's a discipline. And it requires some discipline to have, you know, two or three monitors sitting up there and you see your competitors on the air with a story that is one hell of a good story and you don't have it yet. It takes far more to hold back and say, we don't have it yet, we can't go on with it yet, than to rush on the air with something."

In the Clinton–Lewinsky case, the *New York Times* tried to maintain its traditional role, though it agonized along the way.[7]

For the most part today, however, news organizations have not decided on their role. They operate on a case-by-case basis. Their standards are situational. They may hold to their standards in the first case, but feel a day later that they have no choice but to cover the story or look foolish.

While at first glance this approach may seem the simplest, leaving open the option of making the appropriate choice for each story, in practice, it may create as many problems for news organizations as it solves.

First, it has left many journalists confused, even conflicted, about what they're supposed to be doing. CBS political editor Dotty Lynch said that as she watched network television coverage, particularly that of the twenty-four-hour news stations, she was "sympathetic although sometimes appalled at what's been going on there—names have been thrown out without any verification, without any seeming knowledge of whether it's true or not."[8]

Most newsrooms in practice do not make their standards and procedures all that clear, even to their own staff. CNN, for instance, did not even have someone specifically tasked with the responsibility for thinking about such standards and practices until after its embarrassment over the Tailwind story in July 1998, in its eighteenth year of existence.

If those practices are left to be determined by the situation, the practical effect is that a newsroom will have widely varying standards depending on the reporter and editor, not just the story. Given the thousands of facts to be verified in a newsroom each day, no editing system will make those standards uniform by any criteria.

The situational model also leaves audiences confused. If the news organization does not even know what the rules of proof are supposed to be, how is the audience to know what a given news organization's standards are?

Now add to that the emergence of the Internet as a serious news outlet. In 1998, the Internet grew from being a news deliverer for the computer-savvy to being an important force in breaking news, not just a catalyst as in the case of Drudge, but as a primary deliverer. Indeed a poll by the Pew Research Center for the People and the Press found that more than ever the public turned to Internet sites as a news source during the Clinton–Lewinsky saga.[9]

In the Clinton–Lewinsky saga, the medium became for the first time a major player on a major story. And it moved a step closer to achieving its proponents' goal of becoming journalism's great Jeffersonian leveler—a new world where anyone can be a reporter, editor, and publisher.

The new medium offers unique challenges. It offers the ability to provide constant updates with deadlines that are anything but static.

Like a wire service, news can be "published" on the Web in a moment's notice. But unlike a wire service, many smaller Web sites necessarily lack a second or third pair of eyes to go over a story and ask questions—editorial supervision is often thin.

Even those traditional media that have decided to take up residence on the Internet have found the new medium is full of new challenges. "I am baffled in many cases why newspapers go for the Internet Web site way of leaking news or reporting news rather than just waiting until the next day's newspaper in the good old-fashioned way," NBC's Gwen Ifill said.[10] "It seems like it guards against a lot more surprise and mistakes."

The first question is whether the online version has the same standards of proof as the slower print version of a story. At least that was an issue in the case of the *Wall Street Journal.*

In that case, the *Journal* posted a story on its Web site before the paper had a chance to verify the information, alleging that a White House steward had told a federal grand jury he saw the president alone with Lewinsky. The next evening the Web site softened the story's allegation, saying the steward had told Secret Service agents about an alleged encounter. What was the *Journal*'s motivation for going without verification? "We heard footsteps from at least one other news organization and just didn't think it was going to hold," said *Journal* reporter Brian Duffy.[11]

The *Journal* incident seems a relatively simple question: Is a news organization going to have different standards of proof online than on print?

Perhaps the more difficult case is that indicated by what happened to the *Dallas Morning News* with its story about an alleged Secret Service witness to an intimate encounter between the president and Lewinsky. The paper followed consistent and rather conservative news-gathering standards. Technology put it under a new pressure that old rules could not sustain.

"The story was essentially typeset for the first edition of the newspaper and sent to our Web site at the same time—after meeting all the standards," explained the paper's online assistant managing editor, Dale Peskin. "This occurs about 10:00 P.M. central time at night. When it went out on the Web site, it immediately became news to a lot of people. Indeed, the topic of *Nightline* that very night was the same story, and Ted Koppel began talking with people on his show about this story, as did Larry King. In the course of about a half hour, phones were ringing in both the White House and to one of our sources who provided us with the information. By the end of *Nightline*, the source called [us] back and said, 'Well, I don't think I really said what you're reporting.' So it was a classic case of what we call in the industry, 'source remorse.' After publication, a source changed his mind."

Although there was more than one source for the story, virtually all the crucial material including the key quotes came from one source who changed his mind, a well-connected Washington lawyer.

As a result, editor Ralph Langer concluded in an account published February 1 by the *News*, the paper's policy of having at least two independent sources was "violated." When the main source changed his story after midnight Washington time, "the story was pulled," Langer said. "It was clear that the truth could not be determined before deadlines for our later editions."

"What kind of lessons have we learned about all of this?" Peskin asks. "I think one of the lessons that we learned is the standard for sourcing in old media is not very good, and that standard has changed in our newsroom. We're going to be more careful about that from now on, that maybe two independent sources is not enough, certainly for a story like this. And there's no question about that."

"It also gave us an indication . . . that suddenly we are in a position that information is going to go beyond the range of the delivery truck a lot faster than it travels by print and is distributed to people. That has given us pause to think about what goes online as well, and the impact that both speed and audience have on a story."[12]

7

The Argument Culture

On Wednesday, January 21, the first day the Clinton–Lewinsky story broke in the *Washington Post, Los Angeles Times,* and ABC News, Evan Thomas of *Newsweek* was on *Charlie Rose:*

> I think Clinton likes to tempt fate. He loves danger. I mean, how stupid could he possibly be? You know, he gets elected. He beats the rap. He's in the White House, assuming that this is true, how crazy it is to take up with a twenty-two-year-old girl who's sure to have girlfriends, who's sure to blab about it. It tells you Clinton likes being on the edge. He likes danger. He's been slipping out of jams all his life, and he must get some kind of perverse thrill from it. The question this time is whether it's finally gonna catch up to him.

In the first week of the Clinton–Lewinsky story, fully 41 percent of the statements that came from journalists, either in print or broadcast, were commentary rather than reporting.[1] If you eliminate the Sunday talk shows and *Larry King Live,* incidentally, the number does not change that much, dropping only slightly to 37 percent. That changed somewhat over time. The press moved away slightly from commentary by March, but only slightly. By then 26 percent of the statements in the press (again excluding talk shows) were commentary.[2]

In both cases, roughly a third of all the commentary was unattributed to any reporting whatsoever. It was either the reporter's unsubstantiated opinion, speculation, or judgment.

Incidentally, the numbers could easily be higher. The study did not include two cable channels, MSNBC and Fox, that rely for much of their telecast day on chat.

Much of the vaunted information revolution is not about gathering information but about commenting on it. The basic reason is structural. The rise of the twenty-four-hour news cycle has placed a paradoxical demand on the press to have something to talk about to fill the void. The second reason is economic. The "news hole" of the information revolution has expanded the delivery of information. But the budget for gathering that information has not grown proportionately. In some cases, it has even shrunk.

At MSNBC, a new twenty-four-hour news channel was created, but virtually no news-gathering staff was hired. NBC News correspondents were asked to provide the reporting. Most of the network hires went into staff for talk programs, for bookers to find guests for them, and research staff. The reporting was borrowed from the network.

Journalists acknowledge that they often cross lines on talk shows that they would never even approach in their regular reporting. *Newsweek*'s Howard Fineman told Steven Brill, "[television is] more loosey-goosey than print. . . . It's like you're doing your first draft with no layers and no rewrites and it just goes out to millions of people."[3]

Today, however, the pressure on journalists who appear on talk shows goes much deeper than that. The talk show culture is part of the argument culture. Shows are "cast"—with reporters in an ideological spectrum. On Evan Thomas's appearances on the program *Inside Washington*, they are literally seated ideologically, with Jack Germond and Nina Totenberg on the left and Charles Krauthammer on the right, with Thomas in the middle. Guests are interviewed in advance to make sure the necessary conflict is there, and these programs are designed to push the subject toward conclusion—the way real people talk about things: "OK, but what do you really think, Sam and Cokie?" One of the originating ideas behind the journalist talk show was to capture the feel of the way journalists talked in the bar after work—to say what they couldn't say in print. In the years since, the evolution of the talk show has moved from the polite analysis of *Washington Week In Review* to the predictions and numerical ratings of people and scandals on the *McLaughlin Group* to *Fox News Sunday,* where news makers and news gatherers are cast together, one large group of insiders debating.

The role of the talk show host is often to push guests to cut to the chase, to move it along. Consider Charlie Rose's first question to Ronald Brownstein of *U.S. News and World Report,* who was asked to comment after Evan Thomas:

"Ron, what's the significance of these revelations today? And is this a presidency that may topple because of events that will unfold over the next—"

Brownstein then interrupts to keep his host from going any further: "Well, I think it's getting ahead of it, but it's certainly not inconceivable that, if some of these allegations are borne out ultimately—"

Then Brownstein steers himself back to reporting: "You've had Henry Hyde already saying today that . . . "

Or consider *Larry King Live.* On the first night of the story, the king of talk was pushing toward conclusion: His first question to Bob Woodward was, "Bob Woodward, what crime did the president commit, if he committed a crime?"

The Watergate reporter tries to slow his host down: "Well the hardest thing in all of these scandals is to take something one step at a time, and say these are the allegations. Now what is the proof? . . . These are second-hand conversations."

To Evan Thomas, King asks the first night: "Evan, is [Linda Tripp] a known gossiper about people?"

Thomas clearly has no idea.

To James Carville, isn't this a big story "because [Clinton] has been charged with lying with regard to Whitewater and nobody seems interested?"

Carville: "Well, he hasn't actually been charged."

Then to Bob Woodward: "The story today, Bob, is that we hear Clinton on her phone answering machine?"

Woodward: "There's no indication and again, there's no evidence, that anyone actually has Clinton's voice on some tape or message machine."

What is a journalist to do in this environment? Remaining on TV often means succeeding according to the new values of the medium. Television is now sufficiently critical to a reporter's visibility and stature in Washington that *Time, Newsweek,* and others pay their reporters to make these appearances. It is typical now for newspapers to look for Washington bureau chiefs with a television presence. Larry Kramer, then the editor of the *San Francisco Examiner,* said almost a decade ago of his newly hired bureau chief, Chris Matthews, "I should be paying him out of my marketing budget."[4]

With the advent of the new cable channels since 1996, television is becoming now a critical part of some reporters' direct livelihoods.[5] Several reporters are under contract to networks, at substantial sums. (Fineman was paid "in the ballpark" of $65,000 a year by MSNBC, according to Steve Brill. Isikoff also has a hefty MSNBC contract.)

In effect, the provocative, opinion-laden culture of the talk show has altered the values of print journalism and television generally, creating what Ron Brownstein has called "the culture of assertion," or what Bob Woodward has called "the McLaughlization" of journalism.[6]

This argument culture only adds to the basic commercial reality facing journalism, in which an increasing number of news outlets are competing for smaller pieces of the audience pie. It adds up to enormous pressure on news outlets to have something provocative, something new, to push the envelope, to reach out to new audiences and find younger voices. It is a pressure that would allow an untrained, twenty-five-year-old night law school student named Stephen Glass to become a celebrated young voice at the *New Republic, George, Rolling Stone,* and *Harper's* magazine, in part for his remarkable ability to come up with stunning anecdotal material, even though a variety of outsiders were suspicious that he was making it up.[7]

There is another invisible but meaningful effect on more restrained news outlets from the talk show culture. Editors at *Congressional Quarterly,* for instance, recall cases when reporters were unable to get access to lawmakers because they prefer to spend their time now on cable shows. Unable to ask questions themselves, they pull quotes off the transcripts of these shows, answers to questions posed by Geraldo Rivera, Chris Matthews, Ollie North, or others, rather than by their own reporters. The polarizing nature of the talk show culture thus leaches its way into the other news outlets, even the most serious minded, in more subtle and insidious ways.[8]

Amid a culture of talk, when the story is advancing beyond the facts even the first night, how does a news organization seem cutting edge, up to the minute, comprehensive, while maintaining careful standards?

Often they do not.

"It's now a twenty-four-minute news cycle," says NBC's Gwen Ifill, "and it's one newspapers have gotten involved in as well as the twenty-four-hour networks, so everybody is competing with each other."[9]

In the first week of the Clinton–Lewinsky story, often the most prominent statements in the press were not statements of fact but interpretation. The most common statement by journalists in the first days of the story was interpretive: that Clinton was in big and imminent trouble. In most of these statements, as in the case of Sam Donaldson and Tim Russert, journalists gave the president only a few days or weeks to survive. Most often—more than a third of the time—reporters based this conclusion on their own opinion or speculation. Only roughly a quarter of the time did journalists cite some reporting to support this analysis.[10]

Two of the next five most common statements in the press that first week were also judgmental. One was that Clinton was engaged in double-talk. The other was that impeachment was a possibility.

Though these statements turned out to be accurate eight months later, at the time they were uttered they were wrong, or at least premature.[11] Throughout the scandal, pundits were reaching—and their track record at any given moment was uneven, to put it charitably. At times we heard that the scandal variously would be the end of Clinton, a boon for the GOP, a repudiation of the Christian Right, a triumph for Newt Gingrich. We heard that impeachment would be short-circuited, that a Senate trial would be avoided, and that live witnesses were a certainty. Perhaps more important than the accuracy or inaccuracy of any given prediction is the awkwardness of the press turning public affairs into a kind of Vegas-style game of prediction. There are clear signals that among its reasons for alienation toward the press in this scandal, the public most of all resents the press's penchant for rushing to judgment. Within a few days of the scandal, for instance, a remarkable 80 percent of Americans felt that there was too much commentary in the coverage, according to a survey by the Pew Research Center for the People and the Press.[12]

The tone with which the press cast these statements was often deliberately provocative, shaping the landscape as much as reflecting it. In its February 2 issue, *Time* magazine's cover was, "Monica and Bill: The sordid tale that imperils the president." *U.S. News and World Report* boldly asked on its cover, "Is He Finished?" Even the *Economist*, the British weekly usually known more for its ability to place the news in perspective than its propensity to cry havoc, featured on its cover after the first week a message to Clinton: "If it's true, go."

Is it any wonder the public trusts journalists less as journalists blur the distinctions between themselves and the other actors in the political debate? Journalists, particularly on TV, are often asked to wear different hats on the same story, switching from reporter to analyst to pundit sometimes all in the same five-minute segment. As we saw with people like Tim Russert and Sam Donaldson in the earliest days of the Clinton–Lewinsky saga, the shifting from one role to another can happen so quickly and seamlessly that it becomes hard to distinguish information from speculation and journalist from advocate.

This isn't merely the public being confused by multiple media cultures. The mainstream news organizations are consciously blending the news into a mixed culture with no particular standards. NBC is responsible for the scandal-fixated coverage of MSNBC, the rumor and gossip that pervade the prime-time lineup of Chris Matthews and Geraldo Rivera on CNBC, for the infotainment of certain segments of *Dateline*, and the supposedly more traditional mores of the *NBC Nightly News*. The network news division has become increasingly important to General Electric's profits. In 1998, NBC News earned well over $200 million in operating profit, while NBC overall earned just over $500 million. In 1999, with sports and entertainment struggling because of rising programming costs, the news division may well earn close to two-thirds of the network's profits.[13] NBC News's secret, which has led it to earn nearly four times as much as ABC News and more than ten times as much as CBS News, is that it amortizes its news operations by blurring the distinctions between different kinds of programming. Hence *NBC Dateline* is now an empty vessel into which any style of journalism might fit, borrowing Rivera from CNBC to cover news for NBC, and lending the prestige of NBC News to the televised talk radio format of MSNBC. As the Clinton–Lewinsky scandal wound to conclusion, MSNBC announced it was beefing up its prime-time lineup by using former Nixon speech writer turned TV chat show host John McLaughlin as a news anchor.

Is Michael Isikoff a reporter when he is paid by MSNBC to chat about Lewinsky? What role is Bob Woodward playing as he joins spin doctors like Marlin Fitzwater or Dee Dee Myers on *Larry King?* Is Wolf Blitzer covering the White House when he shares his opinions on CNN talk shows? *Fox News Sunday,* like CNN's *Capital Gang,* combines journalists and politicians in seamless panels of insiders to debate and refer to each other by first name. ABC Entertainment's *Politically Incorrect* moves yet a step further, blending actors, comedians, journalists, elected officials, and political activists into punditry as cocktail party one-liners.

To better understand the argument culture's impact on journalism it might be helpful to look at two of its most vivid exemplars, GOP pundit Ann Coulter and political talk show host Chris Matthews. Both used the Clinton–Lewinsky scandal and television to develop their careers and hone their public personas. In the process they became part of a new class of chatterers who emerged in this scandal. These are not professionals from other fields such as journalism or law who appear on television. Rather, they are a group of loosely credentialed self-interested performers whose primary job is remaining on TV. Unable to rely on experience or expertise, they tend to emphasize qualities in demand in the current climate of television—provocation, polarization, pith, and sex appeal. Their modus operandi increasingly is like that once used to describe New York senator Chauncey Depew, who it was said would launch an army of words that wander aimlessly over the field until it came across a lonely fact which it carried kicking and screaming in its midst until it died of overuse and abuse. With their emphasis on entertainment value, they helped turn the Clinton–Lewinsky affair into a kind of national *Truman Show*, an ongoing television drama that seemed simultaneously real and unreal.

In the process, these chatterers created a new link in the media chain, one that ferried the rumors and innuendo of the ideological extremists and activists into the dialogue, offering companionship and validation to figures like Internet gossip monger Matt Drudge. Despite his early appearances on the *Today Show* and *Meet the Press,* Drudge was largely discounted by much of the media. The Internet provocateur was given his own show on Fox News Network, but most mainstream news outlets did not afford him the opportunity to play latter-day Walter Winchell on their air-time. Even after the Clinton–Lewinsky story broke, most media still didn't take him as a reliable source of information. Drudge's material could work its way into the national consciousness via Jay Leno's monologue, but if it was going to make it into the conversations in the Senate hallways or at office water coolers around the country, it needed to be ferried in by others as well. Coulter and Matthews—and those like them—provided a conduit.

Coulter is part of that pundit class who might be called the cable mavens. If punditry once relied heavily on professional expertise, the rise of twenty-four-hour cable networks has changed that dynamic and expanded the ranks. There is so much air-time to fill, the young bookers who find guests for these programs can no longer draw only on the limited number of experienced experts. Nor is it clear that they would want to. Often young and inexperienced themselves, they watch competing chat shows and increasingly solicit people based on the TV qualities they want, almost as if they were "casting" people to fill roles. Wanting to reach beyond the largely male, middle-aged ranks that had dominated punditry since the days of *Agronsky and Company,* they often opted for young, female, blonde conservatives. But the women they found usually offered little in the way of expertise.

When CNN wanted to attract younger viewers to its campaign coverage in 1996, it picked an attractive blond pollster named Kellyanne Fitzpatrick to become one of its handful of campaign commentators. Fitzpatrick's polling credentials, however, were relatively scarce.

Another new face was Laura Ingraham. A young law associate who was well connected in conservative social circles in Washington, Ingraham gained media attention after she posed with fellow young conservatives on the cover of the *New York Times* magazine, wearing a leopard-print miniskirt. She began appearing on a then-cable show called *Politically Incorrect,* was mentioned in a *Newsweek* piece for being, as one editor there put it, "the fetching fascist," and was hired as one of a team of Gen-X commentators for the launch of MSNBC. She soon became a frequent guest on the popular *Imus in the Morning* radio show, and then quit her legal career to become a full-time television personality, someone who was famous mostly for being famous. Though she is quite bright, Ingraham's appeal owed less to her brief legal experience, her political knowledge, or her influence than to her salty, archly conservative style and her appeal to a young demographic profile. Such skills fit uneasily in a more traditional news context, and Ingraham's stint as a political commentator and reporter for CBS News was short-lived.

Among the new chatterers, Ann Coulter stands out for the stridency of her rhetoric. On programs such as *Crossfire, Rivera Live!,* and *Equal Time,* Coulter called Clinton "crazy," "a horny hick," "a lunatic," "like a serial killer" and "creepier and slimier than Kennedy."[14] It was Coulter who in the first days of the Clinton–Lewinsky saga declared that there were "four other interns" with whom Clinton was involved—an allegation that had been played prominently by Drudge. On another occasion and another show, Coulter said, "I think it is a rational question for Americans to ask whether their president is insane." Her inflammatory style on occasion has hurt her. She lost her position as an MSNBC contributor when she insulted a disabled Vietnam veteran, telling him, "People like you caused us to lose that war." (Coulter claims she did not know the veteran was paralyzed.)

In general, though, Coulter's style goes some of the way in explaining how a thirty-four-year-old woman who arrived in Washington in 1994 to be a low-level $35,000-a-year legislative researcher for a freshman senator, two years later was under contact as pundit for MSNBC. A graduate of the University of Michigan Law School, Coulter had an unremarkable legal résumé as law clerk, low-level Justice Department attorney, and then corporate legal associate in New York. Her portfolio as a rookie legislative aide to Spencer Abraham was limited to a handful of issues such as immigration law.

Instead, she attracted attention for her striking blonde looks and her outspokenness, and when MSNBC started looking for a group of new faces for its Gen-X team, she was among them. Her slights became legendary. When Ambassador Pamela Harriman's casket was being carried off an airplane, she described the Democratic doyenne as having slept her way to the top. To explain the interest in Princess Diana's death, she referred on air to "the pathetic loser soccer moms who just wanted to call in and weep."

Yet in the new world of chatter, being on television gives people standing to write books, rather than the other way around. In 1998, after two years of television exposure, she penned a quick polemic about why the president should be impeached—*High Crimes and Misdemeanors: The Case Against Bill Clinton.* The book quickly shot up the *New York Times* best-seller list. With such section headings as "Kiss It" and chapter titles like "A Cancer on the Country," Coulter's screed was a mishmash of legal and constitutional argument and attacks on Clinton. It delved into a wide array of charges against the president, including allegations that had been dropped by the independent counsel such as "The Travel Office Massacre" and the White House's collection of FBI files, and it did so with Coulter's trademark strong language.

> Instead of Americans' virtues and aspirations, President Clinton reflects the country's dark side. He has debased not only the White House, not only the administration, but the entire country, not only by what he has done, but by how he has defended himself. . . . [C]linton's legacy is that he has no shame, no sense of duty or obligation to the country and no concern for his reputation. O.J. is the model for Clinton's second term.[15]

This section of Coulter's book is indicative of the ways of the new argument culture. It takes statements that many would agree with—"Clinton has no shame," "Clinton has debased the White House"—and piles on other, more flammable statements such as "Clinton reflects the country's dark side" and "Clinton has debased the entire country." It goes on to compare Clinton to a man most consider a murderer, O.J. Simpson.

In ways that are manifest but not unique, Coulter not very subtly employs a rather crass sexuality to help sell her vision of Clinton as first philanderer. Advertisements for *High Crimes and Misdemeanors* used a sultry photo of Coulter with the headline "Bill's Last Blonde." The text below the headline read: "Bill Clinton's worst nightmare just came true . . . Meet Ann Coulter, the constitutional lawyer turned journalist who finally puts the case for Bill Clinton's impeachment to bed."

Such language debases terms like constitutional scholar, but the book and her use of the term "journalist" have allowed her to push allegations into the mainstream media that others wouldn't touch.

Shouters like Coulter alone do not paint the whole picture of the argument culture, however. They require a forum to launch their rhetorical bombs and promote their notoriety. This means the willing involvement of show producers, bookers, and especially talk show hosts, the figures who, as in talk radio, play a central role in the culture of chat. The most notable success story among talk show hosts to emerge from the Clinton–Lewinsky scandal was Chris Matthews, the front man for the five-night-a-week CNBC program called *Hardball*. In 1998, *Hardball*'s audience grew by a whopping 113 percent. By the year's end he was pulling in an average of 612,000 viewers, big numbers for a cable show. One CNBC executive called Matthews "the real success story of last year."[16]

Matthews likes to think of *Hardball* as "a conversation over the dinner table," he said.[17] At Matthews's table, guests get to air whatever is on their mind, often without questioning the facts or asking for substantiation. Matthews's guest list has included Mark Fuhrman, former presidential adviser Dick Morris, and Linda Tripp's book agent Lucianne Goldberg. With guests like that, and a very loose format, *Hardball* became one of the top launching pads for anti-Clinton trial balloons.

Matthews generally manages to not be considered part of the same scandal-peddling cable barker population as Coulter. He's been part of the Washington establishment for more than twenty-five years. Twelve years earlier, the Philadelphia-born, Jesuit-schooled Matthews had a meaningful job on Capitol Hill as communications director to the Speaker of the House, Tip O'Neill. He had come to Washington as an aide to Utah senator Frank Moss and later joined the Senate Budget Committee staff. From there he went on to become a speechwriter for President Carter and later, from 1980 to 1986, O'Neill's spokesman.

Somewhere along the way, he became enamored with the other side of the politician–media equation. He began talking with friends about how he wanted to become a pundit, and he set out consciously to become one.[18] In 1987—before the explosion of cable outlets—that usually meant having journalistic experience, or at least credentials. So Matthews resolved to create some. First, he began writing an insider's book about how Washington works, full of interesting Capitol Hill anecdotes. He called it *Hardball*—it went on to earn both commercial and critical success. Second, he worked out a deal with *San Francisco Examiner* editor Larry Kramer: Matthews got the stamp of respectability he needed in the form of being named the *Examiner*'s Washington bureau chief and a columnist. In exchange, the paper got TV exposure with Matthews and the appearance of being a big-time Washington player. "He needed to be a journalist, to have that kind of respectability on TV. That's what we brought to the table," Kramer said later.[19]

In time Matthews got his own cable show. As time went by, he became more strident, openly sharing his disgust at the president's behavior on air—much to his viewers' pleasure. As the Clinton–Lewinsky saga wore on, he called the president a "louse . . . who's disgraced his office," and at times he even floated his own allegations on his show. On the eve of the House impeachment vote, with *Hardball* going out live, Matthews let loose with a bombshell: a twenty-year-old—and unproven—rape allegation against the president.

The show began with one of Matthews's signature openings: "After a week of shock waves and on the verge of only the second presidential impeachment in American history, the nation's capital is a nervous town tonight. I'm Chris Matthews. Let's play *Hardball.*" But it didn't take him long to bring up "Jane Doe 5"—about seven minutes into the show. A handful of other media outlets might make oblique references to the unsubstantiated charges by the then unnamed woman, but not Matthews. It's a "rape accusation," he informed viewers. Information on the allegation was available to House members at the Ford Office Building, he said, and congressmen were silently using it to make up their minds on impeachment. That, he said, was wrong.[20]

"Help me out here," Matthews said to Tillie Fowler, a Republican congresswoman from Florida. "Why are members of the Republican caucus willing to read material that accuses the president of things like rape and make their decisions based on that information, but are not willing to disclose it after they learned it?"

Fowler explained that House rules prevented it. But, of course, the point was now moot. Matthews just had made it public. Matthews relies on his social connections to woo guests for the show, and on this night his list included prominent Washington journalist, social hostess, and wife of Benjamin C. Bradlee, Sally Quinn. As the group went on to discuss how lengthy the Senate trial might be, it decided that the real problem in Washington was, in Quinn's words, "the lack of civility." Matthews nodded, apparently forgetting that minutes earlier he himself had peddled an unsubstantiated allegation that the president was a rapist.

At a commercial break, Matthews looked at his guests with a smile. "This Jane Doe 5 story is really something," he said.[21]

This is the kind of stuff that makes shows like *Hardball* work—a new angle, however sketchy, on the original, year-old story. It is this approach that pushed ESPN-anchor-turned-newsman Keith Olberman, who had been hosting a companion MSNBC program called *The Big Show,* back to sports. "These shows aren't news. They are the opposite of news," said Olberman, who had moved to Fox Sports Network. "All of these shows are designed to amplify and create an obsession. When the topic is Diana, or even Jon Benet Ramsey, that's one thing. When it's about the government it becomes dangerous."[22]

Matthews saw it differently. He said he was contributing to the public's dialogue about "who we want in the White House. . . . This thing is a national culture war. Nobody made up their minds about Bill Clinton after this. We all knew about him before this. This is about what we think of him. It's town versus gown, and the town is winning."

"All along we have put the focus on the president and what we want from the president. We don't get into the personal stuff. What people are like. We have avoided all the legal talk. It's about the president and who we want in there."

After Clinton's acquittal in the Senate, Matthews tried to analogize the success of *Hardball* to earlier major advances in television journalism. "In its birth, my show is the same as ABC's *Nightline* was," the former spin doctor turned talk show host said. *Nightline* was born during the Iran hostage crisis. They survived. We've been introduced as a program covering one big ongoing story."[23]

Unwittingly Matthews's analogy only highlights how much journalism has changed. *Nightline* began as an in-depth news program designed to provide the latest details and examine in long form specific themes inside a major crisis. It had at its command the entire reporting infrastructure of ABC News. The program always began with a long original reporting segment that laid out the facts and issues. Koppel, a gifted, veteran foreign correspondent, functioned as an interviewer who offered no argument or opinion of his own. The program always relied heavily for its guests on qualified experts or genuine news makers.

Hardball has no grounding in reporting, no basic news function, is not designed to elicit facts or explore issues with policymakers. Matthews's program, and his selection of guests, is grounded in argument. Perhaps more revealingly, Matthews self-consciously sees *Hardball* as populist entertainment. "People aren't tuning me in for news," he says. "They are tuning me in as an alternative to *Friends*."[24]

To understand the role and nature of a program like *Hardball* and its many cousins, consider Matthews's Jane Doe 5 story. It represents a case study of how an unsubstantiated allegation gains relative legitimacy in the Mixed Media Culture. The story originally surfaced on March 28, 1998, when Paula Jones's lawyers filed court documents stating that Clinton had "forcibly raped and sexually assaulted" a campaign worker twenty years ago and then "bribed and intimidated her" to remain silent. The *NBC Nightly News* ran with the story that day, but noted that the woman had recently denied the allegation under oath, and in the days that followed other news organizations discounted the story because of the woman's denial. The story disappeared.

The new journalism of assertion, however, is not a culture dedicated to sorting out whether a story is true. It disregards verification and focuses often on some secondary controversy in order to get the story into circulation. In early December, as the House impeachment vote neared, the story again made the rounds in Washington—pushed by certain members of the House making veiled references with reporters to allegations contained in a locked room that only members could visit. Matthews was the first to air the allegation this time around, and his mention helped give the story new oxygen. House Majority Whip Tom DeLay was quoted in the *New York Times* referring ominously to the contents of the locked room in the House. The supermarket tabloid, the *Star*, on the eve of the Senate impeachment trial, ran the full allegation of rape, including the woman's name. The story was soon receiving prominent play on Matt Drudge's Web site, where the gossip columnist posted in January that NBC correspondent Lisa Myers had interviewed the woman and that NBC was getting pressure from the White House not to air the story. Soon Drudge had shifted the emphasis from the unproven allegations of rape to White House pressure on the press and an internal battle at NBC about whether the story should run.

Then in early February, the rape allegation was aired on Fox News Channel. The *Washington Times* followed, taking a cue from Drudge by running a story not about the allegation but about Fox's story about it. The paper's February 4 story ostensibly was about the way the White House [had] tried to pressure Fox News Channel not to broadcast the story. The *Times* story relied heavily on Drudge as a source, quoting from his Web site. It contained little other information. But the story also mentioned the rape allegation in its lead. Two weeks later the *Wall Street Journal* advanced the story further with a piece on the allegation that was written by an editorial writer and ran on the op/ed page, but read like a news account. The next day the story was fully legitimized when the *Washington Post* gave it front-page (though below-the-fold) treatment. *The Post* lead with the way other organizations were handling the story, but later dealt with the allegation in full. Days later NBC ran its interview with Jane Doe 5, Juanita Broaddrick.

As the Clinton–Lewinsky scandal evolved, there was a subtle but unmistakable shift in the nature of cable news. At least for the moment, the angry and largely conservative audience that during the daytime listened to talk radio hosts such as Rush Limbaugh gravitated during evenings to cable news. Whether this audience will stay loyal to the shows after the story dies down is uncertain. A GOP scandal might have the cable news networks looking for Bob Beckels or Ralph Naders to host programs. But considering the audience demographics in the Lewinsky-dominated world, it made perfect sense that when Olberman left MSNBC the network replaced him with two conservative icons, former Nixon speechwriter turned political pie thrower John McLaughlin and Iran-Contra defendant turned radio talk show host Ollie North. In explaining the move, NBC officials anonymously even adopted the talk radio audience suspicion that the NBC News programming otherwise had a manifest liberal ideological bias. "It's about balance; it's about providing both points of view," one network source was quoted as saying.[25]

Research suggests the public is becoming more discriminating about what is news and what is not. In 1989, for instance, 39 percent of Americans saw the syndicated tabloid program *A Current Affair* as a news show, but by 1997 that number had dropped significantly to 27 percent. By 1997, the majority instead saw *A Current Affair* as entertainment—the number jumped from 28 percent in 1989 to 56 percent.[26]

Yet as the public becomes more discriminating about what is news and what is not, the news media are becoming less discriminating, blurring the lines between entertainment and news in journalism. As the *Today Show*, a program produced by the NBC News Division, got lighter in the 1990s, audiences noticed. The number of people who perceived *Today* as news declined from 48 percent in 1989 to 40 percent by 1997. More significantly, the number of Americans who perceived *Today* as entertainment rose markedly, from 29 percent in 1989 to 40 percent by 1997. Although there is not an enormous amount of data tracking these public perceptions, the numbers we do have suggest that as the so-called mainstream press strays further into infotainment, the public can tell. The press may well be putting its authority at serious risk.

Interestingly, programs that remained more serious were regarded as more serious. While the perception of the *Today Show* is now evenly split between those who see it as entertainment and those who see it as news, the perception of CBS News's *60 Minutes* has remained unchanged. Fully 82 percent of Americans saw the program as news in 1989. Nine years later, 81 percent of Americans still agreed.

The data also suggest that the all-news channels may be shortsighted in filling their schedules with a horde of faceless chat shows.

If the public decides that these shows are lightweight infotainment and not sources of accurate news, then audiences may turn elsewhere when they grow tired of the format, or when events turn suddenly critical and they seek the most authoritative source for information. Emphasizing chat over news may prove to be costly in the long term.

The unceasing void to be filled in the new Mixed Media Culture also causes a second major trend in the press beyond the argument culture. It is the hunger for the blockbuster story. Research by Andrew Kohut and the Pew Research Center shows that the audience for news breaks up into six distinct groups, with no group amounting to more than about 20 percent of the public.

There is a "Mainstream" news audience (20 percent), which has middle-of-the-road preferences, skips the highbrow stuff, reads a local newspaper, watches both broadcast and cable news, and is especially interested in sports and crime but not foreign news.

There is a "Basically Broadcast" (17 percent) audience, those who get most of their news from local TV and some from networks, like prime-time magazine shows, but rarely watch cable news. They're interested in health news, community, and crime, and are more heavily female.

There is a "Very Occasional" audience (18 percent), who tune in only when something really big is happening, and tend to be lower income and heavily male.

There is a "Constant" audience (13 percent), those who watch, read, and listen to almost everything, somewhat indiscriminately. These people watch *Hard Copy* and listen to NPR in about equal numbers. They like all topics and use the clicker.

In contrast, there is also a "Serious News" audience (12 percent), which is more selective, relies heavily on NPR, the *NewsHour with Jim Lehrer*, the *Wall Street Journal*, the *New York Times*, and highbrow news and business magazines.

Finally, there is a "Tabloid Audience" (14 percent), which rejects traditional broadcast news, favoring the *National Enquirer*, tabloid TV, and tell-all talk shows.

Each has different but overlapping interests. But it is difficult, in the context of post–Cold War American society, to find stories that seem relevant to all. Whether a cause or a symptom of declining audiences for journalism, the fragmentation evident in this typology shows how difficult keeping the audience can be.

To overcome the difficulty of cobbling together a diversified newscast with a full menu of interesting material, especially for TV, the trend instead is toward finding the rare story that transcends these audience blocs and attracts people of all sorts: the socko blockbuster story. It is not dissimilar to the "summer movie" theory in Hollywood, finding diverting but not necessarily all-enlightening movie fare that large chunks of Americans will want to see to pass the time. What might that be? Usually something lavish, sexy, and scary: *Armageddon, Deep Impact, Godzilla, Lost World, Independence Day, Waterworld.*

The O.J. case was a journalistic blockbuster. When it ended, networks like CNN that had based their programming around this story were left hungry for another. The fascination with Jon Benet Ramsey might best be understood as this new hungry media culture trying to create another blockbuster. It didn't quite work. Then came Lady Di's death. Afterwards, there was another lull, filled momentarily by stories that seemed to have some of the ingredients, of which sex, celebrity, and violence or sex, celebrity, and scandal are often parts. Momentarily, the Marv Albert trial emerged. By the end of 1997, even these stories had faded from the front pages. "The news has gotten so absurdly good we have to cast our net very far to find the bad. El Nino is about the best we can do," wrote *Washington Post* columnist Charles Krauthammer.[27] Indeed, two of the biggest stories at year's end were the death of entertainer and Congressman Sonny Bono and President Clinton's decision to name the First Family's new Labrador retriever "Buddy."

And then came Monica. The potential of such stories to hold an audience, not a huge audience but a larger one at least than other single stories could hold, is why all news environments like CNN, CNBC, and MSNBC become All Monica Channels, or All Diana, or All O.J. The alternative, to slowly build a newscast or a network that delivers a large menu of news, takes more time, more creativity, and—most important—more money and reporting effort.

If there aren't going to be regular developments, the networks can at least create the illusion of motion by bringing on fresh faces to discuss the story. Each tidbit can be examined, deconstructed, and then quickly submitted to a panel of judges who debate every increment's significance. Does this latest break make a bigger story of a smaller one? What does it say about the fate of the players in the story?

Journalism thrives on big stories. But it survives, ultimately, on proportion. It is the very lack of proportion that has traditionally characterized the supermarket tabloid press. Blowing regular stories into big stories, or big stories into massive ones, means that the rest of the news suffers. That is a failure of judgment and an abdication of the journalist's larger social responsibility to put the news in perspective.

Ultimately, all this has an impact on trust and credibility. Hasty and often faulty prognostications undermine the notion of a useful and reliable press. What is the point of listening to journalists whose interpretation is so often wrong? It may be entertaining but it is not useful. Combined with the inflation of the blockbuster story, whether it is the pseudoinvestigative parade of consumer alert stories on prime-time magazines, or the hyped and inflated microanalysis of Monica–Diana–Jon Benet–O.J.–Tonya, it creates a picture of a press corps lacking judgment or sense. These are journalists who agitate, not educate. You would not trust them as friends. Why trust them as anything else?

If a story comes along that actually merits alarm, the press will probably have a diminished ability to move the public to action. "It's like the boy who cried wolf," suggested Tom Patterson.[28] "That's the ultimate irony of this new journalism. Premised on the media's need to be a vigilant watchdog, it actually undermines that critical function."

The ultimate risk of the press's swing toward the argument culture, however, is not that it undermines journalism but that it undermines society. This is precisely the threat that Walter Lippmann foresaw eighty years ago, when he called on the press to develop a scientific method of verification and precision in his book *Liberty and the News.*

"Where all the news comes second-hand, where all the testimony is uncertain, men cease to respond to truths and respond simply to opinions. The environment in which they act is not the realities themselves, but the pseudo-environment of reports, rumors and guesses. The whole reference of thought comes to be what somebody asserts, not what actually is. . . . Since they are deprived of any trustworthy means of knowing what is really going on, since everything is on the plane of assertion and propaganda, they believe whatever fits most comfortably with their prepossesions."[29]

8

The Press and Cultural Civil War

One of the legacies of the Clinton–Lewinsky scandal is that it deepened public antipathy toward the press. Americans decided quite early they wanted this story over. Within two weeks of the scandal's breaking into the press, a majority (55 percent) thought it would be "the best thing for the nation" to "drop the matter," rather than "carry on the investigation," according to data from the Pew Research Center for the People and the Press.[1] A responsible press couldn't do that. In that regard, there is some element of blaming the messenger in the public anger toward journalists. People didn't like this story and they resented the media for continuing to bring it to them.

Yet as we have documented here the new Mixed Media Culture was also guilty of various excesses in its coverage, and the public sensed this. Anger toward the enormous amount of punditry was the most pronounced source of that antipathy. As cited in Chapter 6 about the argument culture, eight in ten Americans thought there was too much commentary in the coverage of this story. More generally, the public sensed a rush to judgment by the press against Clinton, as if journalists had some investment in the scandal. For instance, they believed that journalists were letting their personal feelings toward Clinton color the coverage. While most Americans were still reserving judgment in early February 1998, seven in ten thought most reporters believed Bill Clinton was lying. More than six in ten (65 percent) thought the press was doing a poor or only fair job of checking the facts before reporting. Six in ten thought the press was doing a poor or only fair job of "being objective." And these numbers were all in the second week of the scandal. The anger would only deepen.

What is also interesting, and often less noted, was that many journalists shared the public's sense of disgust and weariness. It is as if they were strangely entangled in this story. Their professional instincts compelled them to cover it, yet they were repelled by what Clinton had done, by what Starr was doing, by the press coverage, and by the momentum the story developed in the process. One reporter, exhausted by a year of late nights and public anger toward the press, said in exasperation as the story wound down, "I feel like I'm covering the fall of Rome."[2] Said another as he pondered the legacy of Lewinsky for the press and politics, "This feels like the Day of the Locusts."[3] The anger journalists personally felt was not merely a matter of being tired of the story. Reporters often felt this way from the outset. The first week of the scandal, a CNN cameraman returning from a stakeout of Monica Lewinsky turned to fellow riders in an elevator at CNN headquarters and said to no one in particular, "If this girl [Lewinsky] is lying about this, I swear I'll track her down when this is over wherever she lives and hit her in the head with a two-by-four."

Why then did the story develop such velocity in the press? To grasp this, and to fully assess the press's role in the scandal, it is necessary to see the Clinton–Lewinsky scandal in its broader cultural context.

As many have argued, the scandal is at least partly understood as the latest and most traumatic event in an American political and cultural civil war that has raged for more than two decades. Even some of its main actors began to view themselves as soldiers in this larger conflict. "I wonder if, after this cultural war is over that we're engaged in, if an America will survive that is worth fighting to defend," House Judiciary Chairman Henry Hyde argued on the Senate floor, trying to articulate what he thought was at stake in the Senate's impeachment vote. "I wonder if . . . whether there'll be enough vitality left in Duty, Honor and Country to excite our children and grandchildren to defend America." Democrats argued with equal vigor on the other side that they were protecting the presidency from a future in which critics might try to remove any president with whom they disagreed on cultural or moral grounds.

It is beyond the scope of this work to fully trace the origins and outlines of the political and cultural civil war that has dominated American politics for much of the last generation. Yet it is critical in trying to assess the press and the Clinton–Lewinsky scandal to understand the curious and important role that the media have played in this cultural conflict. To do so, some history is necessary.

The roots of the cleavages at play in the Clinton–Lewinsky scandal were seeded in the cultural revolution of the 1960s and 1970s. The upheaval of those decades remained simmering and unsettled, to be played out in revisionist arguments about why the Vietnam War was lost or the effects of language and curriculum in the arguments of multiculturalists. On one side were conservatives who believed that America had set itself on a path of secularism and moral decline, articulated in the writings of such critics as William Bennett or Robert Bork. On the other were liberals who felt that the country had tilted dangerously to the right under Ronald Reagan, becoming cold-hearted and immorally increasing the gap between the rich and poor.

These simmering arguments were then coupled with another major social change, the weakening of the party system in politics. In response to both trends, the two political parties in the 1980s and 1990s increasingly began to define themselves by casting issues like abortion, gun control, or affirmative action as fundamental matters of morality. Democrats created the notion that one's ideas needed to be "in the mainstream" when they attacked Robert Bork's nomination to the Supreme Court and later attacked any proposal to address the critical issue of Social Security reform as a cruel proof that Republicans were cold-hearted.[4] Republicans similarly pressed the question of values by trying to criminalize symbolic acts such as flag burning, and by demanding that candidates swear to an extremist zero-tolerance position on issues like abortion.

In effect, the parties were creating internal orthodoxies not over how to solve the country's most pressing domestic and international issues but over personal thoughts and values. In doing so, they drove the process of politics, and journalism, increasingly away from compromise or solutions. As Robert M. Berdahl, chancellor of the University of California at Berkeley, has argued, elevating political issues to the level of fundamental matters of morality turned them into "issues upon which no compromise is therefore possible." In the process, "the rhetoric [becomes] increasingly moralistic and uncivil."[5]

The reasons behind the cultural drive also had something to do with the mechanics of politics. As traditional tethers between the parties and citizens in the form of ward bosses or church elders weakened in the era of television, both parties were increasingly driven by their outer edges, where the money and activism were strongest. Such cultural issues helped motivate those ideological extremes. These issues, in turn, were also a means for candidates from those edges to win office. When a candidate holds views that are shared by a minority of his or her constituency, politicians learned that often the most effective way to prevail in electoral contests was to make the other candidate seem unacceptable. These cultural divides became known as "wedge" issues because they divided the electorate from one's opponent.

By the 1990s, with the end of the Cold War, still another feature was added to the politics of culture and symbolic wedge issues: a growing focus on personal ethics and behavior. Both parties increasingly began to use personal scandal as a political tool, complete with the arsenal of the ethics probe, the special prosecutor, and the apparatus of special congressional investigative committees. Newt Gingrich emerged from anonymous backbencher to minority whip on the strength of attacking House elders and eventually toppling Speaker Jim Wright in 1989. The media were an integral part of his thinking. (In Gingrich's mind, the arrival of TV cameras in the House and coverage on C-SPAN opening the proceedings to citizens' living rooms leveled the playing field, giving even junior members standing and allowing him to challenge the traditions of the House.) Democrats picked up the cause all the more by trying to prevent Clarence Thomas from taking a seat on the Supreme Court on the basis that he had sexually harassed a worker, which Thomas turned into his own cultural wedge by terming it a "high-tech lynching." The Gingrich approach was combative, his strategic plans laced with military images, and his rhetoric always revolutionary. When he stunned Washington by engineering the first takeover of the House by Republicans in forty years, the white-hot style of talk radio politics he championed consumed the House in both parties.

Journalist Robert Samuelson watched Gingrich's leadership and wrote that Washington had been gripped by "the attack culture." This culture involved, he said, "a mind-set and set of practices that go beyond ordinary partisanship, criticism, debate and investigation."

> What defines the attack culture is that its animating spirit—unexpressed, but obvious—is to destroy and bring down. Does anyone doubt that the assorted Whitewater investigations aim to destroy President Clinton and the first lady? Does anyone doubt that the charges against House Speaker Gingrich were motivated less by ethical sensitivities than the desire to annihilate him politically?[6]

In the end, however, the growing politics of culturalism mainly helped accelerate the voter disaffection it was designed to combat. In their desperate efforts to use marketing strategies to make their parties connect more, and cast issues in compelling emotional and moral terms, partisans on both sides pulled politics away from problem solving and more toward a commercial commodity oriented to its own self-interests. By 1998, at the peak of the Clinton–Lewinsky scandal, voter turnout in the mid-term election reached its lowest point in fifty-six years, despite vast improvements in making it easier for people to vote. As the *New York Times*'s R. W. Apple noted, "the whole political culture of the 1990s, with its criminalization of political conduct and its seeming indifference to important national and international issues, has fallen into disrepute with Americans."[7]

In a sense, the cultural civil war in politics helped create the disconnection between the political establishment and the public that became a central paradox of the Clinton–Lewinsky scandal. While elites, including the media, battled over which party had more moral authority, Americans began adopting a more accepting view of moral flaws and mistakes in their public figures. In part, the battle over morality fed off the public's growing tolerance. Americans seemed to become more accepting of positions once considered morally difficult, such as homosexuality, which activated cultural conservatives on the right. On the left, the trend spurred political correctness, which derided anyone who demonstrated a lack of tolerance. Yet for the majority of Americans, the debate was alienating. Many citizens became more suspicious of broad concepts of moral virtue precisely because political elites began to disagree about them. If elites were quarreling over what was right and what was wrong, then these issues were more open to question. At the same time, the growing skepticism with which the public viewed political leaders gave virtue something of a bad name. Vietnam, Watergate, and an increasingly cynical press had helped undermine how Americans viewed all social institutions over the last two generations. To the degree that the political establishment gravitated into moral debate to reconnect with citizens, it only served to deepen the powerful historical inclination of Americans to see morality, like religion, as a largely personal concern. It was one thing for Oprah Winfrey to talk to Americans about such matters. It was quite another for Trent Lott or Tom DeLay.

The Clinton–Lewinsky scandal was the politics of culture raised to a new and more intense level. Yet its most notable feature may be that it evoked such complex responses. Even as Clinton was being impeached in the House, the lone moment that attracted bipartisan applause came when Minority Leader Dick Gephardt made that very point. "We are now at the height of a cycle of the politics of negative attacks, character assassination, personal smears of good people, decent people, worthy people. It's no wonder to me and to you that the people of our country are cynical and indifferent and apathetic about our government and about our country."

On the surface, the investigation and impeachment of Clinton seemed an expression of neopuritanism. Yet the public's lack of outrage throughout most of the time the scandal dominated the news agenda signaled something more subtle: the degree to which Americans now saw moral behavior as relative. Within two weeks of the scandal's breaking, Clinton's job approval rating had climbed roughly 10 points higher than before the scandal, boosted particularly by an adept performance under pressure at the State of the Union Address.[8] Yet that approval was qualified. While more Americans thought highly of how he was handling his job amid the scandal, fewer approved of Clinton personally.[9] Such numbers suggested a more nuanced and detached perspective on the part of the citizens toward public figures than before.

Perhaps one of the most curious features of the Clinton–Lewinsky ordeal, in turn, is the lone figure who seemed to emerge from it with reputation enhanced. Most Americans saw the saga like a Sam Peckinpah movie of the early 1970s, void of heroic figures.[10] The only one who rose in the public's eye was the woman scorned, Hillary Clinton. After years of being perceived as ideologically too far left and personally too cold, First Lady Hillary Clinton suddenly seemed appealing because she reacted with dignity and stoicism to grotesque public humiliation. In the moral relativism of America of the 1990s, heroism was not a matter of victory of right over wrong, or of solving the nation's problems. Admiration instead came to those who survived betrayal and disappointment in a morally ambiguous world. Clinton in the end emerged more respected for not yielding than either Newt Gingrich or Bob Livingston for stepping down. Even in the arguably simpler world of sport, Mark McGwire and Sammy Sosa are credited as much for surviving the pressure associated with their home run chase as with their batting feats themselves.

The press in this cultural conflict is caught in a no-man's land—a witness, aider and abettor, and victim. It exploits the sensation and conflict of the attack culture and the politics of personal destruction. Yet it injures itself in the process, weakening its ties to the public. The attack culture could not exist without the press. The press, however, would never have engaged in it without the politicians. It has become their co-dependency, their self-destructive addiction.

When speaker-designate of the House Bob Livingston resigned over an anticipated revelation by *Hustler* magazine of his own infidelities, Democrat Jerry Nadler of New York called it, "a surrender to a developing Sexual McCarthyism." Nadler imagined, "a new test if someone wants to run for public office: Are you or have you ever been an adulterer."

Yet the test Nadler imagined might someday come was already here. And the inquisitor is not a senator or congressman seated at a Committee on Un-American Activities. Reporters pose the McCarthy-like question to those who seek public office. And no one even blinks. Livingston himself had been asked the question Nadler anticipated when he first chose to run for Speaker, on camera, by CNN correspondent Wolf Blitzer. The question was considered so commonplace that no one remarked on its being asked, and few made note at the time of Livingston's evasive but thoroughly appropriate answer: "I'm running for Speaker, not Sainthood."

The press contributed to and became an inquisitor in the cultural civil war in ways it never anticipated. In the 1980s, cultural wedge issues that came to drive so many campaigns were effective in part because they were so well suited to the medium of television, with its highly visual grammar and its strict compression of time. Symbolic wedge issues are emotional rather than cerebral, and thus more easily communicated in images than words. For instance, George Bush's highly telegenic presidential campaign of 1988 emphasized his support of the Pledge of Allegiance in schools, his opposition to state prison furlough programs, and his blanket promise of no new taxes. Neither the Pledge nor the furloughs were important issues for

Congress or the president. His tax promise proved too simplistic to be sustainable. But all three made good TV—in part because such visual symbols evoke other unspoken associations for viewers. The Pledge suggested regret over Vietnam, being strong on defense, being culturally conservative. Such symbols are safe, too, because they are vague. One can question points in a detailed plan to solve the deficit. But who opposes the Pledge of Allegiance?[11]

Vagueness is not just a response to the grammar of television or a way to safely attract voters. It is also a response to changes in press practices. The press in the late 1980s and 1990s was becoming more judgmental and interpretative, partly in response to an overstated fear that it had been manipulated by Ronald Reagan.[12] After an early honeymoon, George Bush suffered relentlessly negative coverage during his last two years in office, especially during his reelection campaign.[13] The barrage would only intensify for Clinton.[14] And indeed, his reelection campaign in 1996 became a model of vagueness and symbolism. He ran on such small issues as uniforms for public school children, adding a second day of hospitalization for all new mothers, and a symbolic but largely toothless ban on a few more assault weapons. His slogan, "a bridge to the twenty-first century," was as evocative as but even more empty than Reagan's 1984 slogan of "Morning in America," which at least suggested the economic recovery.

The press also became more engaged in the cultural civil war when it broadened and improved old, narrow definitions of what was news. In the 1970s, as newspapers tried to reflect the changes of the 1960s, they began to cover issues once left untouched. Society and women's pages took on issues such as day care, health, and psychology in addition to fashion and socialite parties. Front pages began to look at stories that probed quality of life, social change, and human interest far more than before, especially in the 1980s.[15] Network news cut back drastically on coverage of politics (though it continued to cover policy at the same level) and turned more attention to quality of life, scandal, and human interest questions—far more, research makes clear.[16] The move toward redefining news accelerated after the end of the Cold War, as news holes once devoted to international areas of conflict with the Soviet Union were turned over to domestic concerns. The media's new attention also made it easier for interest groups focused on issues of values and culture, such as the Family Research Council on the right or People for the American Way on the left, to have an increasingly influential role in shaping the public debate.

The move toward investigative reporting after Watergate, too, created scandal coverage as a genre of journalism that largely did not exist before. A study of the press in 1997 versus 1977 shows that scandal stories increased from 2 percent of the network news, weekly news magazine, and major newspaper stories in 1977 to fully 13 percent of all stories in 1997.[17]

Political scientist James David Barber's book *The Presidential Character* was extremely influential among political journalists of the time. Barber argued that Richard Nixon's character had, as Watergate made obvious, been a vitally important aspect of presidential behavior that the press had failed to take into account.

In addition, the move toward journalism focused on culture rather than policy debate can be seen in the style and points of view of journalists from one generation to another. In an earlier era, Anthony Lewis developed a consistent ideological point of view for the *New York Times* from the left, while William Safire prided himself on constructing a similarly coherent ideological argument from the right. James Reston focused on policy and comity from a vantage point in the center. A generation later, Maureen Dowd writes about politics and the presidency not so much from an ideological or policy point of view as that of cultural critic, evaluating the mores and tastes of the Bushes and the Clintons. Her viewpoint is less about argument than about tone. Her vantage point is less ideological than idiosyncratic. Even a new liberal voice in the *Times*, Frank Rich, while consistent in his partisanship, is a former theater critic whose perspective on the public debate is more culturally than policy oriented. Other columnists, such as Michael Kelly of the *National Journal,* are also principally concerned with questions of morality rather than policy.

Finally, the press took on an even more central role as a conduit of cultural McCarthyism of the 1990s when it began to take over the role of vetting candidates' personal behavior as a criterion for judging their fitness for public office. The seeds of this change, ironically, were planted in the effort to reform the political process in the early 1970s. In the days of strong parties and machine bosses, political insiders in the back room vetted candidates' personal and moral behavior. The bosses decided who would run, who would get money and backing. After the turbulent 1968 conventions, the two parties entered into serious political reform, changing the rules that allowed the conventions to be dominated by local party operatives who were uncommitted delegates, free to declare for any candidate they wanted at the nominating conventions. The reforms meant that the nominations would be decided instead by democratically held state primaries and caucuses, and nominating conventions became ceremonial affairs. Suddenly, the smoke-filled room was all but gone. Decisions about candidates' private lives could no longer be handled in private. The political culture had to find another way to vet the personal side of politics. Gradually, reluctantly, the job fell to the press. The standards changed slowly. In 1976, House Ways and Means chairman Wayne Hays's extramarital affairs were not made public until it was discovered that the lady in question was on the public payroll—and couldn't type. In 1974, Wilbur Mills's drinking was not a public concern until it got so bad that he landed in the Tidal Basin with a stripper named Fanne Foxe.

That wall shattered in 1987, with Gary Hart. The press made a collective decision that there was something reckless about Hart's sexual conduct that spoke to his public character in a subtle but clear way. But many journalists took pains to make a distinction in 1987 that this was not a question of adultery but of character. At the American Society of Newspaper Editors convention the week the story broke, Reg Murphy, publisher and editor of the *Baltimore Sun,* explained, "Most people here don't give a damn about whether Gary Hart is an adulterer, they care about his judgement."[18] The distinction, however talmudic it might seem now, was considered so crucial at the time that people were actually shocked when Paul Taylor of the *Washington Post* asked Hart in a press conference a few days later, "Have you ever committed adultery?"

Taylor's question may have merely put into words what the *Miami Herald* had already asked in its actions, but it swung the door open. Within months, reports filtered within newsrooms of local reporters' asking local candidates the same question Paul Taylor asked Hart. In many of these cases there was no behavior by the candidate to provide a basis for the question—assuming the question was appropriate.

The press was groping, uncertain. As it inched into the bedroom, it created an opportunity for the tabloid press to become relevant. Thus five years later, in the next presidential election, rumors of Clinton's sexual past were rampant. Reporters openly debated whether to probe, and when a woman who had denied having a past with Clinton took money and changed her story (Clinton has since acknowledged having an affair with her), Clinton's history of infidelity, too, became part of the campaign. By 1996, some serious reporters had come around to a new standard. They would investigate sexual history of candidates and determine its relevance. If it were cogent, they would break it. If it were not, they would leave it alone. If some other news outlet, be it a supermarket tabloid or not, broke the story later, they could decide the truthfulness and relevance of the story and act accordingly. Thus when reports surfaced late in the 1996 campaign that Bob Dole had conducted an affair decades earlier, after his first marriage was crumbling, the *Washington Post* reported that it already knew it and had deemed it unnewsworthy. The *Post*'s leadership on this demonstrated the degree to which a news organization that acts first rather than reacts can still set an example. The rest of the mainstream press largely followed the *Post*, and the long-ago affair was a nonevent in the campaign.

What is most interesting, however, about the sexual McCarthyism of the new cultural civil war is that as the press became more aggressive about sex, the public became more accepting. Infidelity in 1987 disqualified Gary Hart. By 1992 it was not enough to disqualify Bill Clinton, despite his admission that he had made mistakes in his marriage. Voters distinguished between the failures of Bill Clinton's private life and what it perceived as the failures of George Bush's public character.

By 1998, grotesquely predatory sexual behavior by Clinton no longer disqualified him from office in the public's mind. Nor did lying about it under oath in a legal proceeding. Infidelity did nothing to damage the fortunes of Henry Hyde or Dan Burton. Livingston's resignation notwithstanding, the evidence suggests that the public has deemed infidelity largely irrelevant—for the moment.

The odd feature is that the political and media establishment are not in synch with that sentiment. As it has grown larger and more diverse, the press has become less a cohesive force in society and more a force of fragmentation. In part, the new Mixed Media Culture is able to more clearly reflect different segments in society, different values and points of view. In doing so, however, it also has lost its ability to point out for people the common ground in society, to note the points of potential compromise, and in that sense to be the forum for bringing the culture together to address and solve problems.

This is partly a function of the economics of news, with its proliferating outlets and ever narrower targeting of audience. It is in part also a function of the traditional norms of news, which tend to build stories around conflict and change. Finding the common ground may also be more difficult because the culture is simply more fragmented.

Whatever the reasons, the contradiction between the press's social and economic interest in creating community and its growing tendency to reinforce fragmentation is a profound dilemma for the news culture. In part, the growing perception that the press is disconnected from the public it serves can be explained through this contradiction. The public has an inchoate sense that its social needs in community are not well met by the press's increasing role in reinforcing social fragmentation. Perhaps more important, the shrinking ability of the press to act as a force of social cohesion threatens to undermine its ability to provide leadership or authority, or to serve what is arguably its most important social function—being a forum for society to come together and solve its problems.

In ways that most in journalism have yet to come to grips with, the press today has a long-range economic stake in compromise and cooperation, a stake that the media's current investment in fragmentation and polarization undermines. If citizens look at public debate and the political process and cannot find their own more moderate feelings reflected—and see few of the real problems in their lives being solved—people will have less stake in using the media. In that sense, the press has a fundamental investment in the political process. And since the political process was designed by the Founders, through its checks and balances, to depend on cooperation and compromise, perhaps the press's most fundamental purpose is to both educate the public about where the points of common ground are and to be a forum for that cooperation. Arguably, moreover, the press's role in acting as a forum for compromise and cooperation has only grown in the modern era, as television and the media in general have replaced the old political apparatus of parties, ward bosses, and community meetings as the principal link between citizens and the political process.

In this light, the press's role in the Clinton–Lewinsky scandal is more deeply disturbing and ironic than it might seem at first. Not only is the press's performance in this drama not a sudden or temporary change but an inevitable and long-building culmination of various trends, the scandal itself has roots in deeper political currents. It is more damaging to the press than many journalists realize. It also will be more difficult for the press to alter course in reaction to the wake of the Clinton–Lewinsky saga. The public has become alienated not only by politics as cultural civil war but by the press's role in that conflict, which the press has not fully recognized or come to terms with.

9

What Is to Be Done

Many of the problems journalists face in the Mixed Media Culture stem from fear of being scooped and lack of preparation. The speed with which stories break means traditional news organizations are forced to make decisions more quickly now than they have ever been. This is different from the days when news services such as United Press International coined the term "a deadline every minute." The news services were mostly relaying their always-breaking information to other journalists, who sorted through the varying accounts and cobbled together their own stories, which they bylined, "From Wire Services." Today, in effect, the pipeline goes straight to the citizen. The journalist is playing the role more of conduit. The citizen increasingly functions as the editor.

In newsrooms, conversations about the ethical implications of a news decision—which could once go on for hours—now often have to be made in a matter of minutes. If one network or newspaper had gotten the Clinton–Lewinsky story, as Doyle McManus pointed out at a forum of the Committee of Concerned Journalists, "we all would have taken two or three days walking around desks and arguing with each other." But because several outlets had the information, the paper was "busting through all of these walls" on ethical questions, every twenty minutes.[1]

In today's competitive mixed-media climate, the days when a single newspaper had time to take two or three days arguing over a story are clearly over.

That limited shred of deliberation, and the relatively closed circle of journalists making the decisions, insulated the press from having to fully explore the limits of its role. In effect, journalism was a tautology. Journalism was whatever journalists did. Often, we defined ourselves by a set of techniques. We will or won't pay for sources. We will or won't use the first person "I" in stories. We rarely had to think through such questions as, what is journalism? or, what is our First Amendment responsibility?

Today, buffeted by technology, competition, economics, the rise of pseudonews, and the decline of audiences and resources, these fundamental questions are now on the table. What is journalism? What is not? How are journalists to react?

There are no easy answers, of course. The problems described here were brought on by large social, economic, and technological shifts.

Yet for all of the difficulties that it seemed to present, the Clinton–Lewinsky saga in the end reinforces, not repudiates, the oldest values of journalism. Close reading of the Clinton–Lewinsky coverage and where the mistakes were made reveals the problems that beset those who strayed furthest from high standards of proof and accuracy, not those who aspired to maintain them.

After the *Starr Report* was issued and journalists sat to consider their mistakes and their triumphs, *New York Times* bureau chief Michael Oreskes came to just this conclusion:

> There is an old piece of advice I think every young reporter in a good news room gets: Do your own work. And I think the lesson of this whole thing for reporters comes down to some pretty simple standards like that one. That's what worked here. The people who got it right were those who did their own work, who were careful about it, who followed the basic standards of sourcing and got their information from multiple sources. The people who worried about what was "out there," to use that horrible phrase that justifies so many journalistic sins, the people who worried about getting beaten, rather then just trying to do it as well as they could as quickly as they could, they messed up. It's amazing really how some simple virtues are re-proven by this whole thing. I think fundamentally the people who tried to do it themselves and did their own work came out of this fine.[2]

Easier, perhaps, said than done. How are news organizations in this new Mixed Media Culture free to simply do their own work? We believe there are steps to doing so, steps that we think can renew credibility and, ultimately, protect financial health.

To begin with, news organizations have to recognize the major shift in how they will have to appeal and brand themselves with the public in this new, more competitive news culture. In the future they will be less able to distinguish themselves by the speed of their reporting, the depth of their information, or the cogency of their interpretation—especially as we move toward electronic instant delivery of print. The perpetual news cycle will synthesize virtually all new reporting and comment into a kind of constant blend, with information an increasingly abundant commodity. Those first with a new fact or insight will have their exclusive only for an instant.

Instead, newspapers, magazines, Web sites, and television stations increasingly will have to distinguish themselves—and establish their brands—by what they choose to report on and the values and standards they bring to their journalism.

Some will publish only what they know is true. Others will publish rumor and innuendo to have the most startling and comprehensive account. Some will separate information carefully from opinion. Some will separate fact from fiction. Others will blend them into a kind of infotainment.

Those who want to maintain historic standards of journalism will have to make them explicitly part of their identity. How?

There are three steps, and each needs to be carried out carefully in advance and requires hard thinking about what a news organization stands for. They require, among other things, much stronger newsroom leadership than managers may be exhibiting at the moment.

Step One: Each news organization should do a great deal more to decide in advance what its news values and policies are.

What, for instance, is your policy about printing unsubstantiated rumors or reports from other news organizations you cannot verify? What is your policy on carrying wire service stories that do not meet the standards you insist on for your own reporters? Will you print everything but try to help readers sort it out? Or will you say, we will print here only what we believe is true—the more classic definition of journalism?

When is the sexual behavior of public officials relevant? What is your policy on using anonymous sources? How many do you need to go with a story? When do you use them, and what is the test for believing what they say? If it changes case by case, why, and how do you communicate that to your readers?

What are your guidelines for reporters' shooting from the hip when they are on television and radio? Are they allowed to say on a talk show what they would not be allowed to write in your paper or say on your newscast? When does analysis become punditry? When does punditry become advocacy?

The questions are no longer academic. They affect each news organization's credibility and therefore its bottom line. As journalism changes, taking on multiple shapes, each news organization in effect must decide what kind of journalism it is practicing. As we will explain, we no longer believe news organizations have the luxury of deciding case by case, in effect veering in different directions.

The critical element here is that news organizations must do this in advance. They cannot wait until the story is on them. If they do, they will fail to have the time to think things out clearly or coherently, or to have the kind of internal debate in the newsroom over these policies and ideas that is necessary to their succeeding. The new media culture had placed journalistic standards into the world of the quick and the dead. Organizations have to know their rules on the vast array of issues that arise when a story breaks, or risk having no standards at all—or standards that are so low they might as well be nonexistent.

Step Two: The news organization must make it clear to those who work there that these are the values in place. Journalism is part art, part literature, and very little science. Reporters are motivated by the values of the institution and by a sense of mission. They need to know what the mission is to thrive.

Sandra Mims Rowe, outgoing president of the American Society of Newspaper Editors, recognized this issue in her speech at the group's convention in 1998.

> In many newsrooms standards are unclear or, given recent evidence, wildly inconsistent. Editors routinely talk about the gap between the journalistic values they hold most dear and those they think guide the reporters they work beside. They worry whether they can hire people with the skill and breadth and understanding to do the job. Reporters say they don't get the journalistic support they need from

> their bosses. They wonder whether their editors have sold out journalistic values for business ones. They long for the inspiration provided by leaders with abiding passion for the gritty world of journalism.
>
> If newsroom values are out of whack or reporters and editors are out of touch with each other and with their communities, whose responsibility is that?
>
> It is ours [the editors].
>
> In some companies, the talk has shifted to financial and marketing imperatives to such an extent that journalists have concluded their owners are blindly driven by Wall Street, unconcerned about the quality of journalism. . . . But if editors are too weary for the fight, too weighted down with their own faded ideals, who will raise high the journalistic flag within today's media giants? We must.[3]

Rowe is articulating what a handful of others in the press are also recognizing. The crisis in journalism in part is a failure of leadership by those who would lead in the newsroom.

Most journalists, we believe, would probably welcome clear guidelines. Too often when a competitor breaks a story, the reaction at a newspaper or network is to damn the torpedoes and charge ahead without a lot of thought to any larger perspective. Editors feel the heat from management. Reporters feel the heat from editors. And eventually rules are bent or sometimes snapped to keep up with a rival. Guidelines help reporters and editors understand how they should conduct themselves in pursuit of a story.

Step Three: Once a newsroom has defined its journalistic standards and values and genuinely made them clear to its reporters and editors, it must then make these values clear to the audience.

In effect, a newsroom must make a covenant with the public about what it stands for.

This covenant is critical. It is the only way for the audience to fairly judge what it thinks of a news organization. It is also the only way for journalistic values to matter to the bottom line.

For much of the public, journalism is not a diverse, multifaceted organism, it is a single entity—the media: *Oprah*, the six o'clock news and the *New York Times*, the tube and its array of channels.

If organizations announced their standards to their audiences, they would be differentiating themselves from the pack. They would be giving readers and viewers specific reasons why one set of coverage is more trustworthy than others.

Finally, if a news organization feels it needs to deviate from its standards and values on a given story—to change its policy on using a single anonymous source, for instance, because the source is truly impeccable—explain why somewhere in the paper or telecast that day.

Each news organization must take these steps individually. The First Amendment is built on the notion that we will have a diversity of voices and styles in the press. Codifying practices for the press at large defeats the purpose of the First Amendment. That does not mean, however, that journalists cannot or should not identify common principles and values. But practices are another matter, and increasingly, trying to impose industry standards of practice on a rapidly changing and diversifying craft is bound to fail.

There is also, of course, no way for rules to take every situation a media organization will face into account. There are going to be times when hybrid situations come up that fit under no particular guideline, or situations where an editor is sure the information he has is solid and wants to trust his gut. Navigating those will be easier for the work done on the issues the organization has worked through. The situational, chaotic nature of journalism, in other words, is precisely the reason why journalists need to think these things through ahead of time.

This kind of branding by values is nothing new. A century ago, as publishers began to free their journals from political parties, they established themselves by enunciating their principles, declaring them in front page editorials, inscribing them on buildings, adding them to their nameplates. Adolph Ochs wanted to distinguish the *New York Times* from the yellow journalism of Hearst and Pulitzer, which he considered seamy. The paper's marketing slogan became "All the News That's Fit to Print," which meant—quite plainly to New Yorkers of the 1890s—unlike all that unfit news in the yellow tabloids. Ochs wore his journalism values on his sleeve, and that was a key part of his business strategy.

Ochs's *New York Times* helped put an end to the yellow journalism of the late nineteenth century both because he created an alternative model that would prove more lucrative and because the immigrants of the 1880s had become more assimilated by the turn of the century and aspired to more middle-class values.

Other cycles of tabloidization similarly passed away because of social change coupled with self-conscious effort on the part of journalists to raise standards. In the 1920s and early 1930s, post–World War I disillusionment combined with the economic explosion of pent-up consumer demand created a self-celebrating generation that turned away from foreign news and policy discussions and made Walter Winchell and gossip columns its fare. Radio technology challenged newspapers as the source of first resort for news.

In that earlier mixing of media there was a rapid plunge down-market. The cynical, give-the-suckers-what-they-want journalist of the "Front Page" was a fair representation of much of what was going on in that time. But as the Great Depression spread and the American people had a vital and vested interested in reliable information about forces they dimly understood that were affecting their lives, they returned to knowledgeable news sources.

It was a recognition of the need to help a confused and fearful public that informed the creation of the Nieman Foundation at Harvard. Charged with the mandate to "promote and elevate standards of journalism in the United States," Harvard's president decided the most important thing he could do was to help journalists become better prepared to cover the complex and difficult stories of the time. What better way than to give them access to the disciplined learning possible during a full year at Harvard, he imagined. Given the tabloid nature of much of the press of that time, however, and the economic concerns of the press owners, Harvard president James Conant was uncertain whether the program would survive its first year. It was, he told his friends, "a dubious experiment." Who, he thought, in the current climate will let their best reporters take a year off from work to study at Harvard? Conant was surprised. The first year's class (1937–38) was flooded with applications. Not only reporters but editors and publishers realized that the turbulent times demanded that they equip themselves to provide the public the most accurate, reliable account of the forces that were sweeping through society.

In one form or another, similar programs at Stanford and Michigan; the Poynter Institute in Florida; the American Press Institute in Virginia; the Freedom Forum centers in New York, Nashville, London, and Hong Kong; and many other education-based journalism training programs helped drive the move upward in professionalization and seriousness of purpose that defined the post–World War II era of journalism.

In the 1960s another generation of celebrated editors helped elevate journalism through force of will, if not written declaration. Ben Bradlee of the *Washington Post,* Abe Rosenthal of the *New York Times*, Gene Roberts of the *Philadelphia Inquirer,* Tom Winship of the *Boston Globe,* Dick Salant of CBS, and Roone Arledge of ABC all made a point of picking fights and using their positions to define their values. They were loud and brash, and their newsrooms followed them.

Their successors are quieter, and the newsrooms they lead less certain of their path. Whereas Abe Rosenthal was avid about speaking out on press controversies, his successor as executive editor at the *New York Times,* Max Frankel, was cautious. A few weeks after taking over, Frankel was contacted by the *Los Angeles Times* for comment on a momentary controversy involving the press. Frankel's secretary returned the call and asked that the questions from the reporter be put in writing. The day after that, she called again to say that Mr. Frankel had decided not to comment. The first time the same *Los Angeles Times* media reporter called Leonard Downie, Ben Bradlee's successor at the *Washington Post*, for comment on some controversy, he similarly demurred, explaining candidly that he was uneasy being an outspoken advocate. This is not intended to imply criticism of either Downie or Frankel. On the contrary, it may have been prudent in the short run not to have engaged in battles. Unlike their predecessors, who in the 1970s were looked up to as leaders of a unified profession, by the late 1980s they may no longer have felt comfortable acting as spokesmen for a profession that was beginning to change and diversify.

But the notion that journalists should not define themselves lest they invite plaintiffs' attorneys or be accused of group-think is not only anti-historical—ten years later, it is also misplaced. For one, plaintiffs' lawyers are increasingly using the lack of public knowledge about a news organization's standards as an opportunity to define those standards themselves—in front of a jury. For another, the press has become so diversified that articulating what one stands for is the only way to create an identity distinct from the lowest common denominator. If you do not disassociate yourself from Chris Matthews or Ann Coulter, how is the public to know? Perhaps more important, if journalists do not begin to speak for the values they believe in, how is the public to believe or credit them?

Silence, far from suggesting self-confidence in one's values, suggests that journalists no longer believe in what they are practicing. To that degree, the fear among journalists of articulating their goals and aspirations in codes or credos only deepens public suspicion of the press. Consider, for instance, how those from other professions see this attitude among journalists that they should never explain and never complain. The University of Missouri Journalism School faculty recently asked Washington attorney and former Missouri congressman James Symington to deliver a lecture on journalism to students. He prepared by attending a panel discussion by prominent Washington reporters. Symington was surprised by the vehemence of the panel against the notion of articulating professional aspirations in some kind of canon. Ever practical, the journalists on the panel, which included CBS's Bill Plante, *Washington Post* assistant managing editor Karen DeYoung, and *Los Angeles Times* reporter Sam Fulwood, contended that such codes, canons, and oaths were often observed only in the breach and thus provided no assurance of appropriate behavior.

"Equally true, it could be said, of such other fragile attempts to influence conduct, as the Constitution, the Ten Commandments, and the Sermon on the Mount," Symington countered. Yet "each is a tether to high purpose." If unreachable goals are as distant as the stars, Symington argued, "the stars are what we must sail by. . . . If the print and electronic media have suffered any diminution of public respect, it may be in part because that crowd senses the absence of a governing principle, any set of granite guidelines to chart the course of news gathering, dissemination, and commentary other than the bottom line demands of what it properly perceives as a business."[4]

Ultimately, the question is larger. "If history, as someone has said, is a race between education and disaster," Symington asked, "do journalists have an active role in the education process itself?"

Other thinkers throughout American history have contended that high aspirations by the press are necessary for democracy to survive. No less a figure than Joseph Pulitzer, who transformed his papers after the years of yellow journalism, contended, "A cynical, mercenary demagogic press will produce in time a people as base as itself."[5]

Yet it might be argued with equal force that a healthy democracy is ultimately the best business strategy for a healthy press, as well. A base people ultimately will turn away from journalism to amusements that are more purely entertaining. Long ago, Harvard president Charles William Eliot argued, "In the modern world the intelligence of public opinion is the one indispensable condition of social progress."[6] Social progress may also be the one indispensable condition of journalism. Hence journalists are not merely victims of changing taste. They are also its architects. Wiser men had seen just this in earlier times of torment. Abraham Lincoln talked about the pragmatic self-interest of taking responsibility for one's own fate in his 1837 address to the Young Men's Lyceum of Springfield, Illinois. He was talking about national security, but in the information age, that security may be more internal than external. "If destruction be our lot," he said, "we must ourselves be the author and the finisher."[7]

The problem of the new Mixed Media Culture is, at least in part, a crisis of conviction. The remedy, or the first step toward it, is to create an antidote to that loss of confidence. The antidote is a renewal of faith. It will require an intellectual rigor journalists have often lacked, and a tough self-confidence about sticking to guns that journalists have not often demonstrated. But at least it is an antidote that is simple to identify: Decide what you stand for. Articulate what you stand for. Then practice what you preach.

Will such an antidote have curative power? In the end, that depends more on citizens than on journalists. If citizens value accuracy, balance, proportion, these qualities can succeed in the news. But it is not preordained that they will succeed. Journalists must first believe in them—and provide them—before citizens can pass judgment on them.

The oldest value of news is to provide people with information they need in a manner that is useful for enhancing their understanding of the world. The best journalism is the most efficient, because it relies most heavily on what is essential and leaves out what is not. It avoids wasting people's time by keeping things in proportion to their meaning. It avoids wasting people's time by only telling them what is true and reliable. It avoids irritating people by deceiving them or mixing advertising and news, or news and propaganda.

Those values have prevailed over time, with cyclical moments of greater sensationalism, particularly in periods of large social upheaval. There is every reason to believe they will continue to prevail, enhanced by technology rather than diminished by it. Yet whether serious journalism survives, first, is up to those who aspire to call themselves serious journalists.

Appendix 1

THE CLINTON CRISIS AND THE PRESS: A NEW STANDARD OF AMERICAN JOURNALISM?

Released Wednesday, February 18, 1998

From the earliest moments of the Clinton crisis, the press routinely intermingled reporting with opinion and speculation—even on the front page—according to a new systematic study of what and how the press reported.

The study raises basic questions about the standards of American journalism and whether the press is in the business of reporting facts or something else.

As the story was breaking, the two-source rule for anonymous sources was not dead, but it was not the rule.

Sources and Attribution for all Reporting

	%
2 or more named sources	1
1 named source	25
2 or more anonymous sources	13
1 anonymous source	8
Reporting attributed to other media source	12
Journalist analysis	23
Journalist punditry	18
	100

A large percentage of the reportage had no sourcing.

The study, designed by the Committee of Concerned Journalists and conducted by Princeton Survey Research Associates, involved a detailed examination of the 1,565 statements and allegations contained in the reporting by major television programs, newspapers and magazines over the first six days of the crisis. The goal was to find out what this cross section of the news media actually provided the American people and what the level of verification was.

Among the findings:

* Four in ten statements (41% of the reportage) were not factual reporting at all—here is what happened—but were instead journalists offering analysis, opinion, speculation or judgment.

* Forty percent of all reporting based on anonymous sourcing was from a single source.

* Only one statement in a hundred (1% of the reporting) was based on two or more named sources.

* News organizations that had better sources generally relied less on analysis and opinion in their reportage.

In a finding that may account for the widely reported public complaint that journalists rushed to judgment, the most common statement by journalists was a conclusion—that Clinton was in big trouble. That interpretation was reported even more often than the core allegations against the President, his denial and the ensuing investigation. The next two most common statements by journalists were also conclusions: that the President was dissembling and that impeachment was a possibility. From the first hours, journalists had, in effect, placed judgmental statements like quotation marks around the core fact on which the story was based.

As the story unfolded, the reliance on named sources and factual reporting tended to rise and the level of commentary and speculation dropped. But that also highlights the insistence to jump to conclusions, especially by news organizations that have the fewest facts.

The study raises such questions as: What are the standards for American journalism in this newly competitive atmosphere? Are we watching them change? Was the standard in the early days of this story, "do we think it's true?" or was the standard "how can we get it in?"

OTHER OVERALL FINDINGS

Looked at another way, the picture that emerges is of a news culture that is increasingly involved with disseminating information rather than gathering it. For instance:

* If the amount of punditry and unverified reporting passed along from other news outlets is added together, it reveals that nearly one in three statements (30% of what was reported) was effectively based on no sourcing at all by the news outlet publishing it.

* Only one in four statements (26%) was based on named sources (overwhelmingly one named source).

* The rest, 23%, was what we called analysis—that is, interpretative reporting attributed to some sourcing so that the audience could evaluate its credibility.

* The fact that almost half of all the reporting was punditry and analysis may be one reason the public is irritated with the press. Public opinion polls such as those by the Pew Research Center for the People and the Press showed that 80% of the public felt there was too much commentary in the coverage.

SOME DISCOVERIES

* In all, 21% of the reporting was based on anonymous sources. Given the nature of a story involving a grand jury and an ongoing investigation, that may not be so surprising, and some of this reportage three weeks later holds up well.

In general, however, the track record of stories with multiple anonymous sources appeared far stronger than those with one.

For instance, weeks later one story that stands out for being unproven—that Monica Lewinsky kept a blue dress stained with DNA evidence of an affair—was initially based on a single anonymous source.

Nearly a week after the blue dress story was first aired on ABC and then repeated in several news outlets, including the *New York Times*, the FBI reported it had found no such evidence. It is possible today that such a dress exists and perhaps even was returned to Betty Currie, the White House secretary, according to yet another anonymously sourced story.

Yet this also may be a textbook example of consider the source. ABC described its source as "someone with specific knowledge of what it is Monica Lewinsky says really took place." In a subsequent interview with the *New York Daily News*, Linda Tripp's literary agent-friend Lucianne Goldberg, a woman with a history of antipathy for Clinton and for engaging in dirty tricks for the Republican party, openly said that she was the source for the blue dress allegation. "The dress story? I think I leaked that." Goldberg told the *Daily News*, laughing in a way that suggested she was mocking the press with this and other leaks. "I had to do something to get their (the media's attention). I've done it. I'm not unproud of it."

* Overall, the press often did little to offer audiences a hint of the possible bias of anonymous sources that might have colored the reliability or completeness of what they were leaking. This was particularly true in some of the stories that remain unverified. One such story, for instance, is that a White House steward told the Grand Jury that he had witnessed an intimate encounter between Lewinsky and the President. The *Wall Street Journal* attributed the story simply to "two individuals familiar with (the steward's) testimony." Similarly, another story that remains unproven was an ABC report that more than one White House staffer, perhaps secret service agents, witnessed an intimate encounter between Lewinsky and the President. ABC attributed this story simply to "several sources."

Many of the anonymous sources in this crisis—even those close to events—might have had an axe to grind and needed to be treated with greater discretion than many of the stories demonstrated. In general, indeed, the press tended to make information look better sourced than it was.

* When one news organization broke an especially controversial story

that others couldn't confirm, there was widespread tendency by other media to pick it up without verifying it. The day after ABC reported the blue dress story, for instance, the percentage of reporting attributed only to other news organizations spiked to 18%, the highest single day in the study.

* Sometimes journalists seemed fascinated with the most salacious details, even if unverified, such as the meaning of oral sex or the background of Monica Lewinsky. On the *Today Show* January 22, for instance, Matt Lauer repeatedly tried to get *Newsweek*'s Michael Isikoff to admit whether he had "heard anything" about a semen stained dress. Even after Isikoff said an answer would be irresponsible, Lauer pressed him, for the third time. "You're not telling me whether you've ever heard of it?"

WHAT WE LOOKED AT

The study measured a snapshot of the news media culture in the first week of the story. From Wednesday, January 21, through Saturday, January 24, we studied the nightly newscasts, prime time magazines and specials, and relevant segments of *Larry King* and *Charlie Rose*, *Nightline*, the morning news shows, the front page coverage of the *New York Times*, *Los Angeles Times*, *St. Louis Post Dispatch*, the *Washington Post*, and the *Washington Times*. Added to that universe, we studied the Sunday network talk programs and the Monday news magazines, *Time* and *Newsweek*.

Based on ratings, influence, and the degree to which their work found its way into other reports, these outlets represented a fair picture of how Americans learned about this story. Indeed, because we wanted to study those outlets that presumably were doing original reporting or interviewing, we deliberately did not include local television, the most popular news source, in the study.

In order to most thoroughly and accurately record press performance, the study did not measure just stories, since some contained more than one key point. It measured instead the key assertions inside stories. Thus in a piece stating that Monica Lewinsky alleged having sexual relations with the President and that Clinton denied the allegation, these two statements were measured separately.

The goal was to find out what the news media was actually providing audiences. How much of the coverage of this story was **factual reporting**—here is what happened? What was the **level of sourcing** for that reporting? How much was **analytical**—that is, analysis attributed to some reporting or evidence in a way that the audience can evaluate how it was arrived at?

How much fell into a different category—one you might call **punditry?** We included here three categories of assertions. 1) **Opinion**, which is analysis not attributed to anything. 2) **Speculation,** which is opinion based on facts that do not yet exist. 3) **Judgment**—an unequivocal assertion that leaves no room for dissent—Clinton is a liar, Clinton cannot survive.

When it comes to analysis or punditry, the study measured what journalists themselves asserted, not what their sources or TV interviewees had to say.

WHAT THE PRESS REPORTED

The most common statement by journalists in the first days of the story was interpretative: that Clinton was in big trouble. Most often—more than a third of the time—reporters based this conclusion on their own opinion or speculation. Roughly a quarter of the time, journalists offered this as an analysis but cited some reporting to support it. Only 17% of the time did journalists cite named sources for this conclusion. Eleven percent of the time it was cited to another media source.

The second most common assertion—that Clinton denied the allegations—was usually attributed to Clinton himself in interviews he had granted.

Given the limited number of reporters who actually had listened to the tapes or interviewed Linda Tripp, most news organizations did not have any confirmation of the major allegation that drove this story—that Lewinsky had talked about having an affair with Clinton and the possibility of lying about it. In only 4% of cases was that allegation attributed

The Top Allegations by Sourcing

	Named	Unnamed	Other Media	Analysis	Punditry	Total
Clinton is in big trouble	17 %	15 %	11 %	23 %	34 %	100 %
Clinton denial	75	5	0	12	8	100
Lewinsky alleged sex and perjury	4	32	30	32	4	100
Lewinsky talking immunity with Ken Starr	30	20	7	32	12	100
Clinton is dissembling	17	6	19	25	32	100
Impeachment is a possibility	43	4	6	8	40	100

to a named source. In more than six in ten cases it was attributed to other sources or offered as part of an analysis. In a third of the cases the news organization offered anonymous sources for that statement.

The fourth most common statement in the first week was that Lewinsky was negotiating for immunity with Kenneth Starr's office. Due in large part to the visibility of Lewinsky's attorney, this was most often attributed to a named or anonymous source. A third of the time it was analysis.

The next two most common statements were particularly judgmental: that Clinton was engaged in double talk and that impeachment was a possibility.

When it came to impeachment, four out of ten times that statement was attributed to a named source, making it one of the hardest sourced allegations in the study. An equal amount of the time it came from reporters offering their own opinions, speculation or judgment.

As for Clinton dissembling, the most common basis for that assertion was a reporter's own opinion, speculation or judgment, about a third of the time. A quarter of the time reporters offered some attribution for that analysis. In one out of five cases it was attributed to a named source. Another one out of five times it was attributed to another news outlet.

FACTUAL REPORTING

Overall, 59% of the reportage was factual reporting—it described what had happened. This reporting had several levels of verification: from multiple named sources, to a single anonymous source to another news outlet.

Looking just at this universe of factual reporting, substantially less than half, only 43%, was based on named sources.

More than a third, 35%, was based on anonymous sources. Another 22% was unverified by the news outlet reporting it and instead was taken from some other news outlet.

Thus, in all, more than half of the universe of factual reporting, 57%, was based on anonymous sourcing or another news outlet.

INTERPRETATIVE REPORTAGE

Clearly, at least in the first week of this story, it was not always the rule to leaven interpretation with evidence that would allow the consumer to assess how much the reporter knew. Roughly half the time, there was no evidence offered. The lines between opinion and analysis were not closely observed in the news pages or the news programs.

Overall 4 in 10 statements by journalists were interpretation (everything from attributed analysis to speculation). Of this interpretative universe, slightly more than half (55%) was analysis attributed or supported by some reporting, thus allowing the consumer to assess its credibility.

The rest, 45%, might be called punditry—that is, the interpretation was not supported by any sourcing. Broken down, 18% of all interpretative reporting was opinion; 21% was speculation (opinions about events that had not yet happened); and 5% was judgment (unequivocal conclusions by the reporter that left no room for disagreement—the president is a liar, the president cannot survive).

NEWSPAPERS

The *Washington Post* was the most aggressive of the newspapers studied in using anonymous sources—including a single anonymous source. Only 16% of its reporting in the first few days of the story was based on named sourcing, significantly lower than the average. On the other hand, 38% of its reporting was based on two anonymous sources, and 26% of its reporting was based on a single anonymous source, in both cases more than triple the average.

The *New York Times* was more conservative: In its pages, 53% of the reportage was based on named sources. Less than 8% of its reporting was based on a single anonymous source. At the *Los Angeles Times*, 43% of its reportage was based on named sources, and 9% on a single anonymous source. The *Washington Times* based 36% of its reportage on named sources and 3.4% on a single unnamed source. On the other hand, the *Washington Times* was also more subjective in its reportage. It published more than double the amount of analysis of newspapers (23%) and more than double the amount of speculation (6%).

Attribution and Sourcing by News Genre

	Named Sources	*Multiple Unnamed*	*Single Unnamed*	*Other Media*	*Journalist Analysis*	*Journalist Punditry*	*Total*
Newspapers	36 %	26%	12 %	12%	12 %	3%	100%
Magazines	23	9	5	8	41	16	100
Evening News	23	19	7	6	32	13	100
Morning News	20	9	10	21	22	18	100
Sunday Shows	27	4	3	11	15	40	100
Prime Time	21	3	7	12	42	16	100
Nightly Talk	10	3	7	27	10	43	100
Nightline	35	8	15	17	8	17	100

NETWORK TV

There were notable differences between networks, as well. CNN had the lowest level of reporting based on named sources, 18.5%, versus 22% at NBC, 24% at ABC and 26% at CBS.

CNN also stood out for allowing its reporters to engage in opinion unattributed to any reporting whatsoever. Nearly 30% of all their reportage was opinion. That is higher than any other network, or any other genre of news outlet.

On its Sunday program, CNN *Late Edition*, 26% of all statements journalists made on the program were unattributed opinions, more than double any other Sunday talk program other than the *McLaughlin Group* (which was 25% opinion). *Late Edition*, however, did not engage in any speculation or judgment. Thus, when opinion, speculation and judgment are factored together as total punditry, *Late Edition* had the lowest percent of statements (remaining at 26%). *The McLaughlin Group* had the most statements that were total punditry (68%) followed by *Meet the Press* with 42% punditry.

On its nightly newscast, CNN *The World Today*, similarly, the level of unattributed and opinion and speculation was double that of any other evening newscast, 15% opinion and 10% speculation.

ABC's *Nightline* was the most factual news outlet of all those studied. More than 76% of all statements on *Nightline* were factual reporting. It had the highest level of reporting based on named sources of any TV show, 35%, and also one of the higher levels of reporting based on a single anonymous source, 15%. While it engaged in less analysis and punditry, *Nightline* also tended more often than other news outlets to air reporting from other news organizations it had been unable to verify itself, 17%.

The single most aggressive news organization when it came to relying on a single anonymous source was ABC News. Across all its programs, 14% of ABC News reporting was based on a single blind source. That compares with 8% for all the news media, and is double any other TV network. Of all news outlets studied, ABC News's *Good Morning America* relied on a single blind source 22% of the time, nearly triple the average. Prime time news magazines were the most analytical genre of program and had the least reportage based on named sources; 42% of what journalists said on such programs was analysis, and 21% of what they reported was based on named sources.

There were also distinct differences between evening network newscasts. CBS *Evening News* was the most judgmental (5.6% versus 2.6% at ABC's *World News* and 0% at *NBC Evening News* and 0% at CNN's *The World Tonight*).

THE SUNDAY SHOWS

The Sunday shows relied far more on speculation, judgment and opinion than the rest of the press. In all, four in ten statements on the Sunday shows were opinion, speculation or judgment by reporters offered without any attribution as to what the reporter based that opinion on, more than double the press generally.

The *McLaughlin Group* defies categorization. Nearly 70% of what appeared on that program was punditry (25% opinion, 36% speculation, 7% judgment). That is nearly double the level of punditry on either nighttime talk shows like *Larry King* or Sunday talk programs like *Meet the Press*.

NEWS MAGAZINES

The length of time *Newsweek* had spent working this story, and its access to Linda Tripp and other sources driving it, showed in the study. *Newsweek* had roughly double the amount of reporting based on named sources (30%) versus *Time* (13%) in the first week. *Newsweek* also had less reporting based on other news outlets (2% versus 14% in *Time*).

Perhaps because it had more original reporting, *Newsweek* also had less analysis (33%) than did *Time* (49%).

Looking at a different category, the news magazines were the most aggressive when it came to inferring lessons about Bill Clinton's interior life or psychological motivations in this story. In all of the reporting, for instance, there were 10 instances in which journalists suggested that Bill Clinton had a sex addiction. Six of these occurred in one Monday's editions of *Time* and *Newsweek*.

In general, traditional news outlets tended to invest more in reporting and verification. Less than 3% of the reportage in newspapers, and only 12% on the nightly newscasts was punditry, compared with roughly 25% in all of news media.

DAYS OF THE WEEK

The press tended to leap to conclusions early on this story and then pull back. More than four in ten statements on the first day were either analysis or punditry (43%), declining each day thereafter until the Sunday talk programs, when it spiked upward again. Similarly, the reliance on named sources grew over time, rising from 17% on Wednesday to 36% on Saturday.

METHODOLOGY

SELECTION/INCLUSION OF BROADCASTS AND PUBLICATIONS

Newspapers, magazines and news broadcasts were selected on an ad hoc basis to provide a snapshot of nationally influential media, keeping in mind the importance of audience, ownership and editorial diversity.

Sources and Attribution Each Day of Coverage

	Wed. %	*Thurs.* %	*Fri.* %	*Sat.* %	*Sun.* %
Named sources	17	22	29	34	27
Anonymous sources	26	26	26	17	7
Other media sources	15	16	11	18	11
Analysis	23	17	24	25	15
Punditry	20	20	10	4	41

Newspaper and magazine stories were either downloaded in their entirety from the NEXIS database, publication websites or were clipped from the publication in which they originally appeared. (Note: when the NEXIS database produced similar stories from the same newspaper, but different editions, the longer of the two stories was coded.)

Broadcast stories' transcripts were acquired via network websites or professional transcript services.

CODING

Coders analyzed each news story[1] in its entirety, identifying the *initial* appearance of any individual statement/allegation within that story: these each became a **case.** (A news story was likely to contain multiple statements/allegations, and therefore, multiple cases.) Coders next analyzed all references to the particular case within said story, and the sourcing attributed in each instance.

When a statement or allegation had multiple appearances within one story it was considered only one case. Coders then identified all attribution cited by the journalist, and coded the case on the basis of the highest level of sourcing that appeared.

INTERCODER RELIABILITY

Intercoder reliability measures the rate at which two coders, operating independently of one another, code the same material in the same way. This monitoring occurred throughout the coding process, and no significant systematic errors were found.

Some of the columns in the tables may not add to 100% due to rounding.

---

[1] For talk programs and Sunday shows, news stories were generally defined by commercial breaks. The exception: when the anchor/host went to a correspondent outside the studio or presented a prerecorded piece, that was considered a separate story.

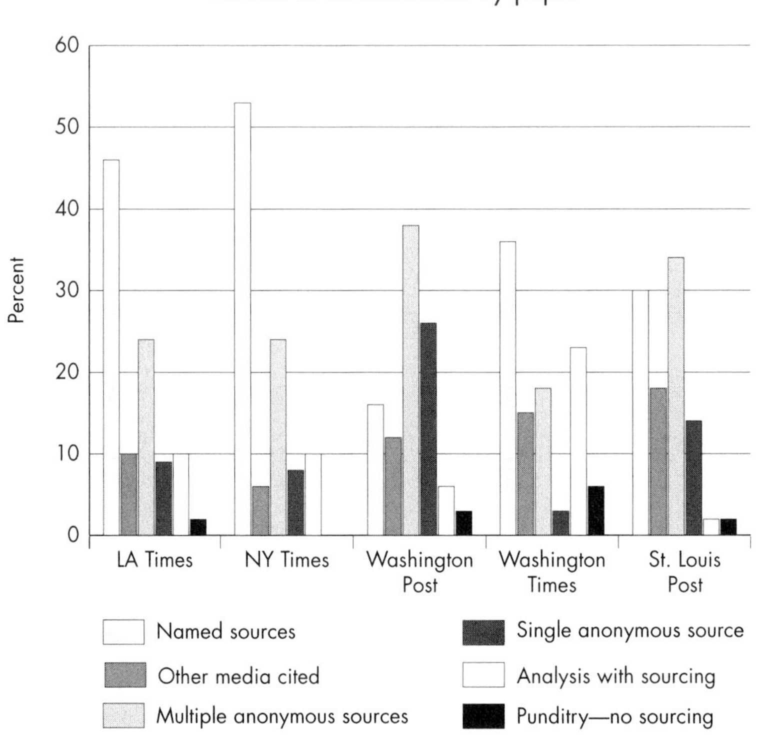

	LA Times	NY Times	Washington Post	Washington Times	St. Louis Post
Named sources	46 %	53 %	16 %	36 %	30%
Other media cited	10	6	12	15	18
Multiple anonymous sources	24	24	38	18	34
Single anonymous source	9	8	26	3	14
Analysis with sourcing	10	10	6	23	2
Punditry—no sourcing	2	0	3	6	2
Total*	100	100	100	100	100

*Numbers may not add to 100 due to rounding

News Magazines: TV and Print

Percent of all statements by program/publication

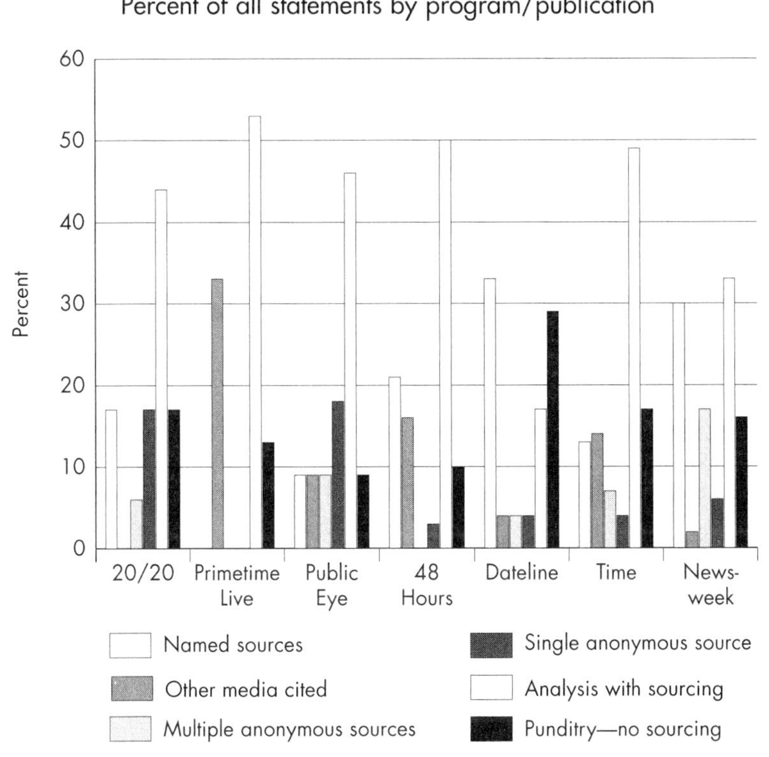

	20/20	Prime-time Live	Public Eye	48 Hours	Date-line	Time	News-week
Named sources	17%	0 %	9 %	21 %	33%	13%	30%
Other media cited	0	33	9	16	4	14	2
Multiple anonymous sources	6	0	9	0	4	7	17
Single anonymous source	17	0	18	3	4	4	6
Analysis with sourcing	44	53	46	50	17	49	33
Punditry—no sourcing	17	13	9	10	29	17	16
Total*	100	100	100	100	100	100	100

*Numbers may not add to 100 due to rounding

TV: Morning and Late Night

Percent of all statements by program

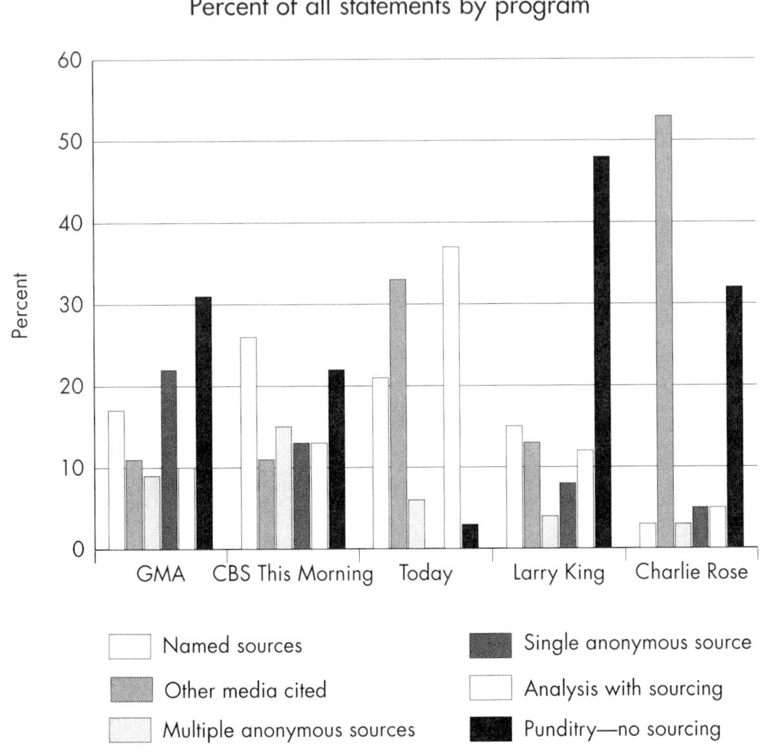

	GMA	CBS	Today	Larry King	Charlie Rose
Named sources	17%	26%	21%	15%	3%
Other media cited	11	11	33	13	53
Multiple anonymous sources	9	15	6	4	3
Single anonymous source	22	13	0	8	5
Analysis with sourcing	10	13	37	12	5
Punditry—no sourcing	31	22	3	48	32
Total*	100	100	100	100	100

*Numbers may not add to 100 due to rounding

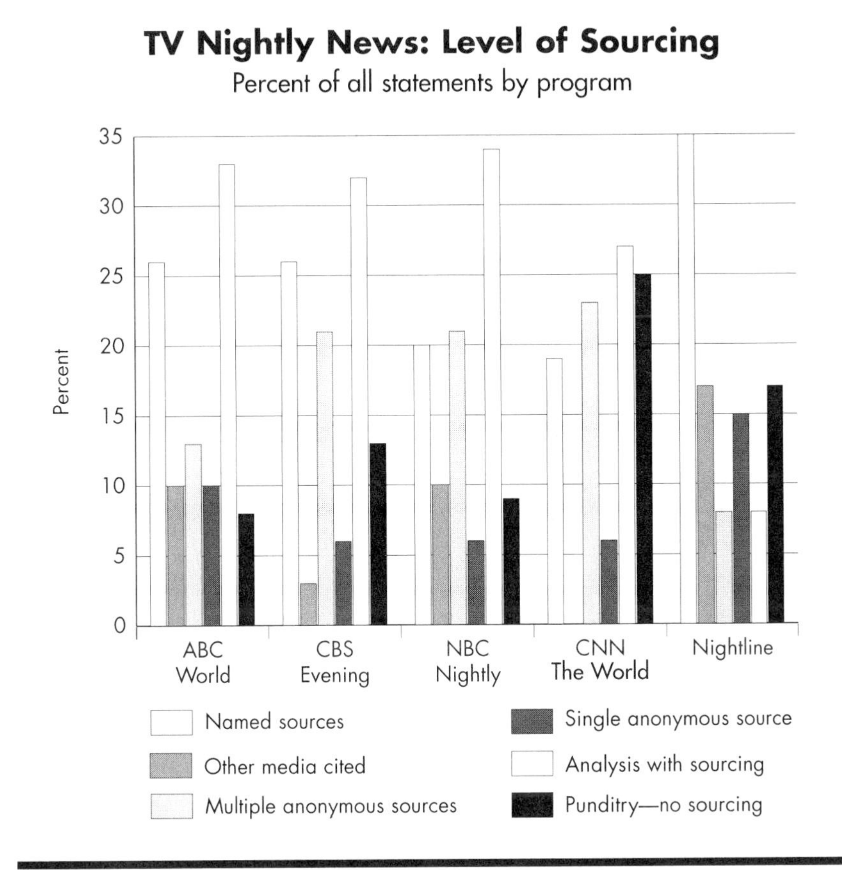

	ABC World	CBS Evening	NBC Nightly	CNN	Nightline
Named sources	26%	26%	20%	19%	35%
Other media cited	10	3	10	0	17
Multiple anonymous sources	13	21	21	23	8
Single anonymous source	10	6	6	6	15
Analysis with sourcing	33	32	34	27	8
Punditry—no sourcing	8	13	9	25	17
Total*	100	100	100	100	100

*Numbers may not add to 100 due to rounding

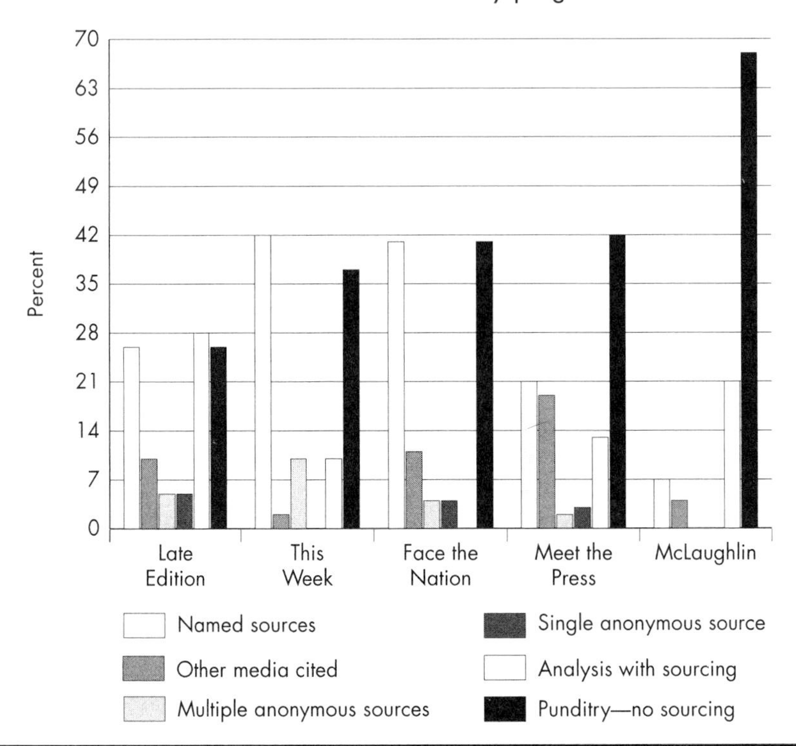

	Late Edition	This Week	Face the Nation	Meet the Press	McLaughlin
Named sources	26%	42%	41%	21%	7%
Other media cited	10	2	11	19	4
Multiple anonymous sources	5	10	4	2	0
Single anonymous source	5	0	4	3	0
Analysis with sourcing	28	10	0	13	21
Punditry—no sourcing	26	37	41	42	68
Total*	100	100	100	100	100

*Numbers may not add to 100 due to rounding

Appendix 2

THE CLINTON CRISIS AND THE PRESS: A SECOND LOOK

Released Friday, March 27, 1998

As a rule, the press has tended to describe anonymous sources in the vaguest terms in covering the Clinton–Lewinsky saga, according to the results of a new study of what and how the press has reported.

Only occasionally has the press offered audiences a glimpse of what the biases or allegiances are that might be influencing what an anonymous source is revealing.

The study, a follow up to an earlier one in February, raises basic questions about whether the press has become too lax about offering readers as much information as possible, and whether journalists have allowed sources to dictate terms too easily.

At the same time, there are signs the coverage over time has moved more toward factual reporting and named sources and away from commentary.

The study, conducted by the Committee of Concerned Journalists, involved an examination of 2,051 statements and allegations contained in the reporting by major television programs, newspapers, magazines and the Associated Press over four days in January and March. For comparison, the study included a list of tabloid publications and television programs. The goal for this, the second part of a study conducted by the Committee in February, was to find out how sources were described, how the mainstream press compared to the tabloids, and how the coverage may have changed by the seventh week.

Among the findings:

* Six in ten statements from anonymous sources in the mainstream media (59% of all anonymously sourced reporting) were characterized in the vaguest terms, "sources said," "sources told our news organization" or "sources familiar" with the event.

*Less than two in ten statements (17% of the anonymously sourced reporting) offered even the slightest hint of the source's allegiances.

*Print was more forthcoming about the nature of its anonymous sourcing than was broadcast.

* The mainstream press' use of anonymous sources was not that different than those of the tabloid press, such as *Inside Edition* or the *National Enquirer*, though the tone of the two different kinds of media, which is not quantified by the study, varied considerably.

CHARACTERIZING ANONYMOUS SOURCES

In the first study it became clear that a key question was how much news organizations were helping audiences understand about anonymous sources—not simply whether the press was relying on such sources.

"Almost everybody we are talking to (on this story) has an agenda, and I don't think we've been very straightforward with viewers and readers on where that information is coming from and how it might be tainted as a result," Dotty Lynch, political editor of CBS News, said at a conference discussing the first study.

Characterization of Anonymous Sources, Jan. 23, Mar. 5&6

	News	Tabloids
Rumors	4%	7%
Sources said	23	30
Outlet has learned	20	3
Source familiar with	16	9
Job characterized	13	17
Bias characterized	17	30
Other	8	4
Total	100	100

So for the second half of the study, we decided to look at how anonymous sources were characterized—including to what extent audiences were given information to judge for themselves if a source might have an ax to grind.

We looked at one day in January and two in March and one week's editions of *Time* and *Newsweek*. We then broke down the characterization of anonymous sourcing into five categories:

—How much was attributed to rumors.

—How much was a blind attribution, "sources said," or "the news organization has learned," without any further identification of the source.

—How much offered even minimal information about how the source would know what he or she was revealing ("a source familiar with the investigation"), but did not signal what if any bias or allegiance the source might have.

—How much described in some manner the source's official affiliation (a Justice Department official, a Capitol Hill source).

—Finally, how much described what side of the dispute the source was aligned with, such as a friend or supporter of the President, a Republican source, or a lawyer for Linda Tripp.

The overwhelming plurality of the anonymous reporting in the mainstream press (43%) was essentially blind. It said simply "sources said," or "our news organization has learned," offering no effective characterization of the source.

Another 16% of the time, the sources were characterized as simply being knowledgeable in a fairly vague way, such as sources "familiar with the situation" or "close to the investigation."

Taken together, that means that 59% of the time the sourcing was quite vague, offering no sense of where the source or sources worked or what slant there might be to the information.

Only 17% of the time did the press characterize anonymous sources in a way that offered at least some guidance as to the sources' allegiances, describing the source as "a supporter" of the President, "a Democratic" or "a Republican source," "a friend" of someone, or someone "close to" someone else.

And 13% of the time, anonymous sources were described in a way that offered a glimpse of where the source worked, such as "a Capitol Hill source" or "a Justice Department source," but did not necessarily offer much guidance as to the source's bias or allegiance.

At least explicitly, the press did not engage much in passing along rumors and innuendo in the days studied. In only 4% of the cases were "rumors" or "it is believed" or similar attribution cited as the source.

Vague characterization of sourcing may be one of the reasons that the public registers irritation with press coverage of this story. Certainly, some anecdotal evidence would suggest that. *Washington Post* ombudsman Geneva Overholser offered voice to some of these complaints in one of her columns. "Sources said, sources said...what sources?" Overholser quoted one reader as complaining. "Just who are these informed sources?" asked another.

The leak of the Clinton deposition may have lowered the amount of blind sourcing captured in the study because so much of the reporting by other media was attributed to the *Washington Post* rather than an anonymous source.

DIFFERENT TYPES OF MEDIA

Print was much more specific about characterizing sources than television.

Newspapers, the Associated Press and the news weeklies used the vaguest characterization of anonymous sourcing—"sources said" or "the news organization has learned"—26% of the time. Television used this blind characterization 68% of the time.

The two media were much closer when it came to describing the potential allegiance or bias of an anonymous source (18% in print, 15% on TV).

Print was five times more likely to characterize a source's job affiliation (25% of the time for print, 5% for broadcast).

One explanation is that in the compressed time frame of television, journalists often forgo identifying sources, since many of those names might not mean much to viewers anyway. The question is whether that standard applies as well to an investigative story, where such details may help viewers judge the story.

Although the universe is not large enough generally to break out individual news outlets, one statistic may be worth mentioning. The Associated Press on the days studied did not characterize the bias of any anonymous sources.

Interestingly, the tabloid press, which in the study included *Star*, the *New York Post*, the *National Enquirer*, *Inside Edition* and *Rivera*, were sometimes more specific in characterizing sources on the three days studied.

Only 33% of the time did they rely simply on "sources say" or "the news organization has learned," more than newspapers but less than the networks.

Nearly a third of the time (30%), the tabloids offered insight into the source's bias. This is no endorsement of the tabloid genre, but rather an indication of where the mainstream press can do better. Often those who skate closest to the edge of sensation know that, for legal reasons, they have to be careful about attribution.

The tabloid press attributed anonymous reports to "rumors" 7% of the time, roughly twice that of the mainstream press.

Sources and Attribution for Mainstream News

	January	March
Two or more named sources	1%	4%
1 named source	24	24
2 or more anonymous sources	15	8
1 anonymous source	9	4
Attributed to other media or leaked Clinton deposition	14	33
Journalist analysis	24	18
Journalist punditry	13	8
Total	100	100

*For the sake of comparison, this chart does not include Sunday talk shows, tabloids, the AP, the *NewsHour* or *Larry King Live*.

HOW THE COVERAGE HAS CHANGED OVER TIME

This second snapshot of the Lewinsky story captured three days in March that may or may not have been typical, but they were dramatic. They were the day that the Clinton deposition in the Paula Jones case was leaked to the *Washington Post*, the day following, and that week's subsequent news magazines.

If you compare the same outlets in January versus March on this story (eliminating the Sunday shows and *Larry King Live* from our earlier January universe because they are not included in March), the news media seemed to be moving more toward the use of named sources and away from punditry, especially at certain news organizations.

In January, more than one in three of all statements by journalists (37%) were either reporter analysis or punditry. In the three days studied in March, the level of analysis and punditry had declined noticeably to one in four remarks (26%).

And this came at a moment, during the release of the Clinton deposition, when the news might reasonably be expected to have called for a fair amount of analysis, or certainly invited a significant amount of punditry.

The shift suggests that at least incrementally the press did react to complaints by the public and critics that the media were getting ahead of the facts.

When it came to what was reported, perhaps not surprisingly, the most commonly reported topics concerned either elements from Clinton's deposition or Vernon Jordan's simultaneous appearance before the grand jury. The three most commonly reported statements involved the leaked Clinton deposition, who asked Vernon Jordan to help Monica Lewinsky, and questions about whether Clinton was dissembling

WHAT WE LOOKED AT[1]

For this second part, the study measured a snapshot of media in the first week of March (six weeks later than its initial snapshot). On March 5 and 6, it looked at the three commercial broadcast nightly newscasts,

[1] We have excluded one program from the comparison here, because the level of punditry by journalists on the show was so extreme that it skewed the numbers of the entire study. To make the comparisons meaningful, we have set it aside as a special case. On the days studied in March, 69% of what appeared on Larry King Live was punditry, amounting to two-thirds of all the punditry encountered in the study.

CNN's *The World Tonight*, prime time magazines, any relevant segments of *Charlie Rose*, *Nightline*, the morning news shows, the front section coverage of the *New York Times*, *Los Angeles Times*, *St. Louis Post Dispatch*, the *Washington Post* and the *Washington Times*. Included also were the following Monday's *Time* and *Newsweek*. The study this time also added the *NewsHour* with Jim Lehrer and the coverage of the Associated Press on March 5, 6 and January 23.

Based on ratings, influence and the degree to which their work found their way into other reports, the goal was to represent a fair picture of how Americans learned about the story.

For the tabloids, the study looked at the edition or broadcast on March 5 and 6 or the corresponding weekly edition of the supermarket *Star*, *National Enquirer*, *New York Post*, *Rivera* and *Inside Edition*. As a basis of comparison, we also looked at the tabloid universe for the week of January 23.

In order to more thoroughly and accurately record press performance, the study did not just measure stories, since most contained more than one key point. It measured instead the key assertions inside stories. Thus in a piece stating that Monica Lewinsky alleged having sexual relations with the president and that Clinton denied that allegation, these two statements were measured separately.

The goal of this second snapshot was to answer three questions: How specifically was the press characterizing anonymous sourcing? Had the coverage changed from the first week of the story over the next few weeks? At a time when people talk about "tabloidization" of the news media, how different was the tabloid press on these questions?

In writing this report, we have excluded one category of news outlets, the Sunday talk shows, that were part of the original January sample so that March and January comparisons can be made. The Sunday talk shows were not monitored in the March sample. As a result, there are some cases where numbers for January vary slightly from those cited in the earlier report.

The study was designed by the Committee of Concerned Journalists and executed by Lee Ann Brady of Princeton Survey Research Associates.

ANONYMOUS SOURCES

There were other shifts in coverage, some of which may reflect the Clinton deposition. The use of anonymous sources, at least during the moment of the leaked deposition, had dropped from 24% to 12%. More specifically, the reliance on a single anonymous source declined from 9% of all reportage in the first week to 4% in the three days studied in March.

Not surprisingly, the reliance on other media jumped from 14% to 33%, clearly because people were citing the *Washington Post*.

TYPES OF NEWS OUTLETS

TABLOIDS

The breakdown of coverage in the tabloid press differed from the more serious press only slightly. Whereas the serious press in March relied on named sources 28% of the time, the tabloid press did so in four out of ten statements (41%).

The serious press relied on anonymous sourcing 12% of the time in March, and the tabloid press did so 21% of the time.

The serious press and the tabloid press had the same amount of analytical reporting in March (18%).

When it came to punditry, the tabloid and the serious press were also not far apart (8% serious and 11% tabloid).

What these comparisons do not capture is broad differences in tone. Because such judgments are often subjective, we chose not to make those sorts of comparisons in this study.

NEWSPAPERS

While most types of news outlets were moving away from analysis and punditry (punditry is defined as opinion, speculation and judgment by reporters not attributed or supported by any reporting) only newspapers seemed to buck the trend, perhaps because understanding the Clinton deposition invited or even required some analysis.

The level of analysis, that is, interpretation attributed to some reporting so that readers could judge for themselves how to evaluate it, rose noticeably in every paper studied, from 12% in January to 19% in the days studied in March.

Some news outlets appeared to change how they were covering the story more than others. *The Washington Post*, which stood out for its aggressive use of unnamed sources in the first week of the story, moved away from that approach somewhat, even while it was breaking the Clinton deposition from an unnamed source.

Its reliance on named sources rose from one in seven statements in January (16%) to more than one in four in March (28%).

In contrast, in January, six in ten statements (64%) in the *Washington Post* came from anonymous sources.

In March, even if you add the leaked Clinton deposition and anonymous source reporting into one category for the *Washington Post* (since the *Post* broke the deposition based on an anonymous source), anonymous sourcing dropped by a third in the *Post* to four in ten statements (43%). Moreover, the leaked deposition accounted for three quarters of that.

Sources and Attribution by News Genre, March 5&6

	Named Sources %	Multiple Unnamed %	Single Unnamed %	Other Media* %	Journalist Analysis %	Journalist Punditry %	Total %
Newspapers	32	8	3	36	19	2	100
Morning news	23	6	1	42	17	11	100
Evening news	31	18	9	16	16	11	100
Print magazines	19	6	10	21	21	23	100
AP wire	34	8	3	44	10	0	100
The *NewsHour*	29	0	0	43	21	7	100
Tabloids	41	12	9	9	18	11	100

*"Other media" includes the leaked Clinton deposition.

The other newspapers studied relied somewhat less on named sources in March than in January, though again this was likely because they were reacting to the leaked deposition story.

THE ASSOCIATED PRESS

The Associated Press was added to the second round of the study because of the degree to which its coverage appeared in radio, TV and newspaper accounts around the country.

In March, the AP relied on named sources about the same as newspapers (34% versus 32% for newspapers), and on anonymous sources the same amount as newspapers (both 11%). But it engaged in less analysis than newspapers (10% versus 19%) and, at least on the two days studied, in no punditry.

Overall, combining the AP coverage studied in both January and March, versus newspapers in January and March, the AP relied more on named sources and less on anonymous sources than newspapers and engaged in slightly less analysis.

Both engaged in only a negligible amount of punditry.

THE *NEWSHOUR*

The *NewsHour* was added to the study because it has some of the most strict rules about the use of anonymous sources and journalists engaging in commentary.

Associated Press, Level of Sourcing

	January	March	Combined
Named sources	61%	34%	51%
Multiple unnamed sources	7	8	8
Single unnamed source	11	3	8
Other media/Deposition	7	44	21
Journalist analysis	12	10	11
Journalist punditry	2	0	1
Total	100	100	100

The *NewsHour* did not use any anonymous sourcing on the days in the study.

When it came to named sources, reporting based on such sourcing accounted for about as much of the coverage as it did on the other evening newscasts (29% versus 31% for the others).

Actually, the PBS program engaged in more analysis among reporters, though this occurred in roundtable sessions rather than taped reports (21% versus 16% for other evening newscasts).

The *NewsHour* did engage in punditry on the nights studied, though less than other evening newscasts (7% versus 11%).

MORNING SHOWS

In the first study, we discovered that morning news programs (*Today*, *Good Morning America* and CBS *This Morning*) have markedly different standards for approaching hard news. They relied less on reporting and more on commentary than the evening news.

That had changed somewhat by March. The level of commentary on the morning shows on this story declined from 40% in January to 28% in March.

More specifically, analysis dropped from 22% to 17%. Punditry dropped from 18% of the reportage to 11%.

PRIME TIME MAGAZINES

The prime time magazines, which leaped on the story in January, had lost much of their interest by March. Even during the extraordinary moment of the leaked Clinton deposition, the three network prime time magazines that aired those nights did not cover the story.

NETWORK EVENING NEWS

The nightly newscasts also shifted in the way they covered the story. In January, 44% of all the coverage was commentary, either reporter analysis attributed to some reporting or outright punditry. In March, even in the wake of the Clinton deposition that might have invited analysis (and did in print), the level of commentary on the evening network newscasts dropped by more than a third to just 27%.

Specifically, the level of analysis on the network nightly newscasts declined from 32% of all reporting in January to 16% in the days studied in March. The level of punditry remained roughly the same, 12% in January, 11% in March.

Comparisons between individual newscasts are unwise here because the coverage had subsided to the point that the numbers of statements studied per newscast are relatively small.

PRINT NEWS MAGAZINES

Time and *Newsweek* also showed some shift in their coverage, at least in the way they covered this story in their March 16 issues from the way they covered it on February 10.

The level of analysis in January was 41%, the highest by far of any type of news outlet. That subsided to 21%. But the level of unattributed punditry rose in *Time* and *Newsweek* over the earlier time frame, from 17% in January to 23% in March. While that increase may not seem large, it is interesting that it is the only type of news outlet to see an increase in punditry.

DOES SPECIFICITY EQUAL QUALITY?

Having a more detailed characterization of sources is no guarantee that a story is accurate. Some stories that have held up well have barely characterized the sources. The *Washington Post*'s publication of the details of Clinton's deposition in the Paula Jones litigation effectively offered no guidance at all about the source—even as to whether it was a person, a document or whether the reporter had watched a video of the interrogation. Yet the level of detail and texture in the story raised little doubt that the reporter had an extraordinarily comprehensive account of the event to work from, and no one has substantially challenged the accuracy of the story.

Stories like the Clinton deposition, however, are fairly unique. Most journalism of this sort comes in drips and drabs, and journalists acknowledge they often rely on the vagaries of instinct and experience to decide whether a source is on the level.

The *Los Angeles Times* had numerous sources outlining Monica Lewinsky's affair with her high school drama teacher days before that story broke, but decided not to publish because "the allegation required a high level of confirmation"—preferably the teacher or Lewinsky themselves—and the paper did not have either, according to the paper's Washington Bureau Chief, Doyle McManus. What's more, there was the question of "relevance," whether Lewinsky's sexual history had anything to do with her potential credibility. The story eventually broke when the teacher went public.

The paper similarly held off running another story that other news organizations eventually went with: the allegation that Lewinsky had a blue dress that contained DNA evidence of an affair with the President. "It was left out because of insufficient evidence," a taped conversation that the paper's reporters hadn't themselves heard, and which may or may not reflect the truth, McManus said.

New York Times Washington Bureau Chief Michael Oreskes recalled a moment when the paper was ready to go with an explosive story about Lewinsky and the President that "several sources swore was true." On deadline, one of his reporters came into his office with a sinking feeling about it. Something about the way the sources were talking made him uncomfortable. Based largely on that reporter's gut instinct, Oreskes said, the paper held off.

The story proved problematic when published elsewhere, and Oreskes credits his reporter for persuading the paper not to publish.

"We've exercised restraint and we're not sorry about it," agreed *Baltimore Sun* bureau chief Paul West, who cited still other cases at his paper.

These examples demonstrate also that the press may have often demonstrated more restraint than is obvious from what the audiences see. Yet public perceptions of press coverage of events may be more heavily shaped by the worst cases than by the best.

How a source might know information and what if any bias the source may have also take on added significance when the source is characterizing an event like a conversation or a relationship where the tone and context become critically important.

Consider the *New York Times* story that implied that the President might have tried to influence his secretary Betty Currie's grand jury testimony.

Part of that story hung on the characterization that the President might have tried to influence how Currie viewed his relationship with Monica Lewinsky by summoning Currie to the White House and "leading her through an account" of his relationship by asking Currie "a series of leading questions" about it.

The White House version is that Clinton was simply trying to judge whether his own testimony had been accurate, so he was checking his recollection with Currie—not trying to manipulate her.

To weigh these different versions, it makes a significant difference whether the sources for the *Times* story, described as "lawyers familiar with (Currie's) account," are working for Currie, Kenneth Starr and Paula Jones or someone else.

The journalist's instinct for full disclosure alone might suggest news organizations should try to offer the most specific characterization of a source possible so that readers have the most information to judge the accuracy of the news.

The fact that news organizations have not done so might suggest that reporters have ceded too much power to sources in negotiating ground rules. It might also suggest that in an increasingly competitive atmosphere, news organizations are willing to bargain more freely to get stories.

But if being more specific about a source would make readers or viewers more skeptical about the story, perhaps because the source might appear biased, that may also be a signal to the news organization that the story hasn't been adequately sourced.

METHODOLOGY

SELECTION OF BROADCASTS AND PUBLICATIONS

Newspapers, magazines, news broadcasts and tabloids were selected on an ad hoc basis to provide a snapshot of nationally influential media, keeping in mind the importance of audience, ownership and editorial diversity. The dates studied in March were selected at random in advance.

Newspaper, magazine and print tabloid stories were either downloaded in their entirety from the NEXIS database or were clipped from the publication in which they originally appeared. (Note: when the NEXIS database produced similar stories from the same newspapers, but different editions, the longer of the two stories was coded.)

Broadcast stories were coded from one of the three sources: transcripts acquired via network websites; professional transcript services; or videotapes of broadcasts.

CODING

Coders analyzed each news story in its entirety, identifying the initial appearance of any individual statement or allegation within that story: these each became a case. (A news story was likely to contain multiple statements and therefore, multiple cases.) Coders next analyzed all references to the particular case within said story, and the sourcing attributed in each instance. When a statement or allegation had multiple appearances within one story, it was considered only one case. Coders then identified all attribution cited by the journalist, and coded the case on the basis of the highest level of sourcing that appeared.

SOURCE CHARACTERIZATION

Each time a statement or allegation had an anonymous source as its strongest level of sourcing, it was then coded to see how the sourcing was characterized.

INTERCODER RELIABILITY

Intercoder reliability measures the rate at which two coders, operating independently of one another, code the same material in the same way. This monitoring occurred throughout the coding process, and no significant systematic errors were found.

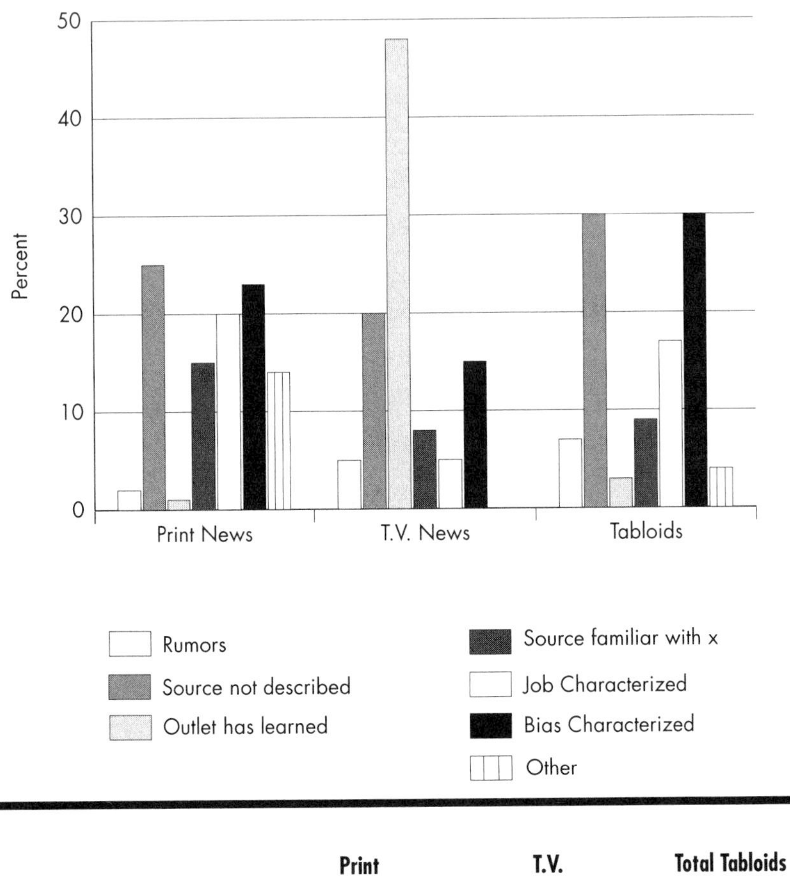

	Print	T.V.	Total Tabloids
Rumors	2%	5%	7%
Source not described	25	20	30
Outlet has learned	1	48	3
Source familiar with x	15	8	9
Job characterized	20	5	17
Bias characterized	23	15	30
Other	14	0	4
Total	100	100	100

Number and percent of anonymous statements by media type:

Print News	88—20% of all statements
TV News	61—25% of all statements
Total Tabloids	76—30% of all statements

To study the characterization of anonymous sources, we created a list of ways the sources were described by the major news outlets. The complete list follows, broken down within the broad categories we write about in the text.

List of Characterizations of Anonymous Sources

Rumors
It's rumored
It's believed

Sources said
A source said
Unidentified source
Source qualified—?
Various sources

Outlet has learned
We (news organization) understand
We have learned/been told by a source/sources
I (reporter) understand
I have learned/been told
I have learned/been told by a source/sources

Source familiar with X
Source close to the investigation
Source familiar with Lewinsky tapes
Source who knows Lewinsky
Someone who knows Tripp

Job characterized
Arkansas State Trooper
Justice Dept. source/official

Job characterized (cont'd)
Pentagon official/source
White House source
White House staff
Capitol Hill source

Bias characterized
Source Close to Starr
Republican source
Democratic source
Supporter/friend of the President
Supporter/friend of Hillary Clinton
Friend of Monica Lewinsky
Supporter/friend of Linda Tripp
Supporter/friend of Vernon Jordan
Clinton's lawyer(s)
Lewinsky's lawyer
Tripp's lawyer
Jordan's lawyer
Jones' lawyer(s)

Other
This a default category for characterizations that did not fit into any of the categories listed above. Any characterization that appeared five times or more was added to the list.

Newspapers: Level of Sourcing

Percent of all statements by paper, March 5–6, 1998

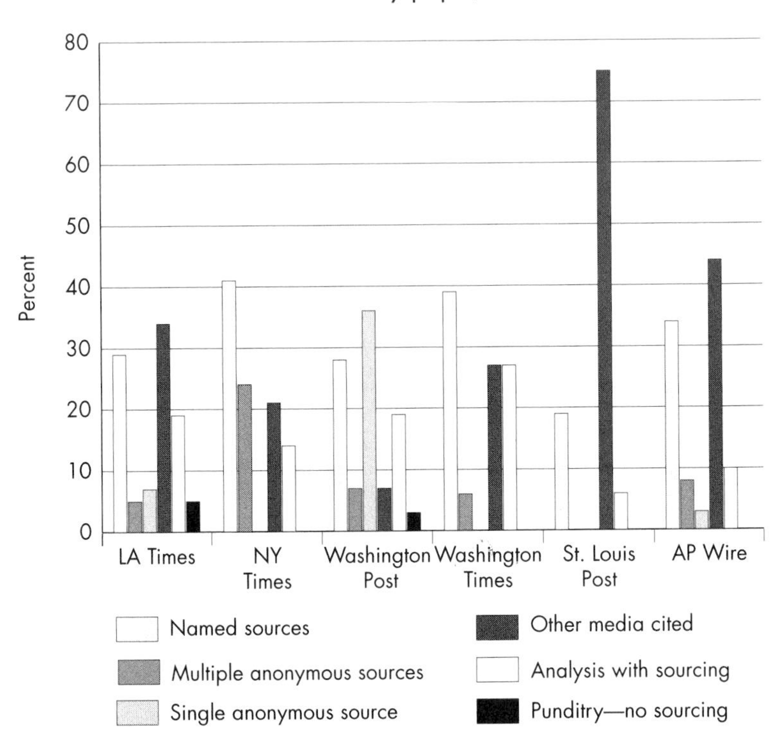

	LA Times	NY Times	Washington Post	Washington Times	St. Louis Post	AP Wire
Named sources	29%	41%	28%	39%	19%	34%
Multiple anonymous sources	5	24	7	6	0	8
Single anonymous source*	7	0	36	0	0	3
Other media cited	34	21	7	27	75	44
Analysis w/ sourcing	19	14	19	27	6	10
Punditry—no sourcing	5	0	3	0	0	0
Total	100	100	100	100	100	100

* For all media except the *Washington Post*, statements attributed to the leaked deposition were included in "other media cited" because they were attributed to the *Washington Post*. For the *Washington Post*, the leaked deposition was a single anonymous source.

Clinton-Lewinsky Study—Phase II[2]
Total Number of Statements or Allegations by News Outlet

	Late January	Early March
Network Evening News		
ABC World News Tonight News	78	19
CBS Evening News	72	8
NBC Nightly News	70	10
CNN The World Today	48	8
PBS Lehrer NewsHour	3	14
Network Morning Shows		
Good Morning America	116	13
CBS This Morning	54	25
Today Show	136	52
Network/Late Night		
Nightline	60	12
Charlie Rose	40	0
Newtwork/Prime Time Mags		
Prime Time Live	15	no broadcast
Public Eye w/ B. Gumbel	11	no broadcast
20/20	18	0
48 Hours	38	0
Dateline	24	0
Daily Newspapers		
LA Times	68	41
New York Times	51	29
St. Louis Post	44	16
Washington Times	89	33
Washington Post	69	58
Print Newsmagazines		
Time	84	36
Newsweek	88	16
AP Wire	95	59

	Late January	Early March	
Tabloid News Outlets			
National Enquirer	28	12	
Star Magazine	28	5	
New York Post	47	34	
Rivera	37	10	
Inside Edition	30	0	
Total	1541	510	2051

[2] In phase II of the study we went back and looked at Jan. 23 again to see how anonymous sources were characterized. We added the Associated Press, the *NewsHour* and selected tabloids to the universe. Then we looked at all of these outlets for March 5 and 6, plus that week's *Time* and *Newsweek*.

Appendix 3

METHODOLOGY FOR THE THIRD LEWINSKY STUDY*

The study identified seven major threads (see Appendixes 4 through 10), tracking their first appearance and subsequent development in major news outlets in print, television and the Internet. The major media outlets were defined as ABC *World News Tonight*, CBS *Evening News*, NBC *Nightly News*, CNN *World View*, the *NewsHour with Jim Lehrer*, the *New York Times*, the *Washington Post*, the *Los Angeles Times*, *USA Today*, *Time* and *Newsweek*. In addition, using the Lexis database, searches were conducted of all available news outlets by key words and concepts to expand the universe. Then other research sources, such as the Hotline, were consulted to further expand the universe.

* This study was conducted by the Committee of Concerned Journalists, a consortium of journalists founded in 1997 from various media interested in reflecting on the performance and responsibilities of their profession. The group is funded by the Pew Charitable Trusts. This study was released October 20, 1998.

Appendix 4

The Blue Dress Story

ABC was accurate in its first reporting that a stained dress of Lewinsky's contained traces of the President's semen. That report cited a single source, who, according to ABC, had "specific" knowledge of what Lewinsky had claimed.

After the initial report, however, the story came under attack by a number of other publications. Various factors may have led the media to discount the story—its potential impact, its unsavory nature, the possibility that Lewinsky was lying and the fact that ABC cited only a single source. But the attacks on the dress story, along with testimony leaks, made it easier for columnists and commentators to downplay the dress story, after it reemerged. It also made it more likely that they could be spun by the White House

In the end, the garment proved to be a critical element of the independent counsel's case. It was physical evidence that an encounter had occurred.

A chronology of stories on the blue dress:

1) On **1/21**, the day the story broke in the *Washington Post*, *Newsweek* goes on AOL with excerpts from the Tripp tapes. In its account *Newsweek* reports Lewinsky "says that Clinton gave her a dress."

2) On **1/21**, the *Drudge Report* wrote "investigators have become convinced that there may be a DNA trail that could confirm Clinton's sexual involvement with Lewinsky. . . . Tripp has shared with investigators a conversation where Lewinsky allegedly confided that she kept a garment with Clinton's semen on it—a garment she allegedly said she would never wash."

3) On **1/22,** Sam Donaldson on *Good Morning America* announced that in his Paula Jones deposition Clinton denied he had a sexual relationship with Lewinsky, but "apparently acknowledged giving her gifts, including a dress." That same day the *Washington Post* reports that Starr is "searching for gifts that might show whether there was a relationship, including reports that Clinton gave Lewinsky a dress."

4) On **1/23,** *ABC* first reported a "semen-stained" dress. "According to a source, Lewinsky says she saved—apparently as a kind of souvenir—a navy blue dress with the president's semen stain on it."

5) On **1/24,** the *New York Times* reported: "Investigators who have heard the tapes said Ms. Lewinsky made references to gifts she had received from President Clinton, including a dress. On one of the tapes, the investigators said, Ms. Lewinsky tells a friend, Linda R. Tripp, that the dress contains a semen stain from President Clinton."

6) On the **1/25** *This Week*, Lewinsky's attorney, William Ginsburg said: "There is a report, which I was advised of initially a week ago by the office of independent counsel, that there was a dress that might be forensically important in terms of DNA evidence." That same day, as Ginsburg appeared on *Meet the Press*, Tim Russert asked Ginsburg about "reports that there may be some dresses or a dress with DNA evidence." Ginsburg: "That's a salacious comment. It's a salacious comment, because I would assume that if Monica Lewinsky had a dress that was sullied or dirty, she would have had it cleaned. I know of no such dress." Russert: "But did they take some of her clothing?" Ginsburg: "Oh, yes. Oh, yes. . . . They took her black and blue pant suits and dresses."

7) On **1/28,** *MSNBC* reported Starr's investigators are "awaiting laboratory test results" on one of Monica Lewinsky's dresses. That same day Ginsburg on *CNN* acknowledged the testing but added "I don't anticipate that they're going to find a thing." *CBS* announced the FBI has "finished DNA tests on one of Lewinsky's dresses. The results are due soon." Later, *CNN* reported "We've been told by sources that all of the garments appeared to be clean, had come back from a dry cleaners, but presumably, they think that if there are any stains, or whatever on those garments, DNA testing might show that, so they're going through that very, very carefully."

8) On **1/29,** the *New York Post* wrote: "The dirty little secret is that some Democrats are quietly crossing their fingers in hopes that

Lewinsky really does have a dress with semen stains so Clinton will have to exit quickly, instead of dragging them down."

9) On **1/29,** *CBS* reported "that no DNA evidence or stains have been found on a dress that belongs to Lewinsky. The dress and other clothes that were seized by the FBI from Lewinsky's apartment after she told a friend that they might contain physical evidence. But again, tonight, the FBI lab has found no such evidence."

10) In its **2/16** issue, *Time* magazine ran a piece on the dress headlined: "The Press and the Dress. The anatomy of a salacious leak, and how it ricocheted around the walls of the media echo chamber." The piece chronicled how the story made its way from Drudge's web site to the mainstream. . . media. The piece said the dress story showed, "the occasional slipups that occur as a story reverberates through today's journalistic echo chamber, changing slightly each time it is repeated."

11) On **6/20,** Lucianne Goldberg told Matt Drudge on *Fox News Channel* that she was the source of stories that Lewinsky had a semen-stained dress: "That's a true story. . . . there's a lot more to that story. . . . Hopefully, when Linda (Tripp) is able to speak for herself we'll know more about a lot of things. . . . Trust me, when this thing hits, it will be explosive, the accumulation of all the things that people don't know yet."

12) On **7/8**, Geraldo Rivera told his audience, "There is, ladies and gentlemen, absolutely no possibility that a so-called semen-stained dress exists because Monica has insisted to everyone that things never went that far, never went to completion."

13) On **7/29,** *ABC* reported Lewinsky will turn the dress over. "Legal sources tell ABC News that as part of the immunity deal with prosecutors, Monica Lewinsky agreed to turn over evidence she claimed would back up her story that she had a sexual relationship with the President. The sources confirmed that one piece of evidence is in fact the dress Lewinsky said she saved after an encounter with Mr. Clinton because it had a semen stain on it. . . . The dress may provide Starr with forensic evidence of a relationship."

14) On **7/30,** the *New York Times* and *Washington Post* reported that the dress will be turned over to Starr. The *Post* writes, "If there is bodily fluid" on the dress, "it would take just a day to determine whether there was enough to submit for DNA testing and just a

few more days to yield a unique genetic marker. . . . Such a test, though, would be meaningless without a blood sample from the president to compare with and it was unclear whether Clinton would agree to provide that."

15) The evening of **7/30,** the blood-test angle received prominent play. *ABC*: "White House sources say there has been no discussion of whether Mr. Clinton would turn over a sample if requested by Starr. It is clear that an ordinary citizen could be compelled to provide such a sample. . . . Starr clearly is hoping that the physical evidence Lewinsky provided, including the dress will prove that Mr. Clinton's sworn statement denying a sexual relationship was false." *NBC*: "A dress containing the President's DNA would dramatically change this case. . .Experts say the FBI lab could know within a day if there's bodily fluids on the dress; tests to identify the DNA could take at least a week. Only if there is a definite DNA finding would the prosecutors consider asking the President for a blood sample."

16) In its **8/10** issue, *Newsweek* reported that Goldberg said Tripp and Goldberg plotted to steal the dress from Lewinsky's Watergate apartment. "We were just two girls having a Nancy Drew fantasy," Goldberg says in the piece.

17) On **8/4,** Geraldo Rivera on his *CNBC* show announced that "one source very close to the president" had told him that "one lab says it's positive," meaning there is human genetic material on the dress. About an hour later, "*NBC* sent out a system-wide computer message warning its journalists not to follow" Rivera's footsteps. The message: "NBC News has not confirmed and will not report the information about test results from *Rivera Live*." Rivera did "back off from one part of his report." *NBC* did not criticize Rivera's account because he "reported what he had heard," but also said, "We were concerned that if it was taken without context, it would take on a life of its own."

18) On **8/21,** the *New York Times* reported that the FBI crime laboratory "has determined that the stain on the blue dress was semen, two officials briefed on the results said."

The Starr Report and supporting documents

The report confirms the accuracy of the blue dress story:

"After reaching an immunity and cooperation agreement with the Office of the Independent Counsel on July 28, 1998, Ms. Lewinsky turned over a navy blue dress that she said she had worn during a sexual encounter with the President on February 28, 1997. According to Ms. Lewinsky, she noticed stains on the garment the next time she took it from her closet. From their location, she surmised that the stains were the President's semen.(1)

Initial tests revealed that the stains are in fact semen.(2) Based on that result, the OIC asked the President for a blood sample.(3) After requesting and being given assurances that the OIC had an evidentiary basis for making the request, the President agreed.(4) In the White House Map Room on August 3, 1998, the White House Physician drew a vial of blood from the President in the presence of an FBI agent and an OIC attorney.(5) By conducting the two standard DNA comparison tests, the FBI Laboratory concluded that the President was the source of the DNA obtained from the dress.(6) According to the more sensitive RFLP test, the genetic markers on the semen, which match the President's DNA, are characteristic of one out of 7.87 trillion Caucasians.(7)"

Appendix 5

The Talking Points

From the first disclosure that Monica Lewinsky had handed Linda Tripp a document entitled "Points to make in an affidavit," many major news outlets emphasized a supposition that turned out not to be provable—namely that the memo was written by agents of the President and represented a smoking gun proving obstruction of justice or witness-tampering.

Talk show hosts and guests speculated about the authorship and the likelihood that the "talking points" represented witness tampering. Several publications printed versions, speculated on the origins and implicated the President, Vernon Jordan or Bruce Lindsey. Those suppositions may have reflected the suspicions of some investigators, but they proved to be unsupportable. After Lewinsky received immunity, several stories reported the "talking points" were no longer considered central to the investigation.

The Starr Report devotes only two non-judgmental sentences and one footnote to the "talking points."

A chronology of the "talking points":

1) On **1/22**, *Newsweek* disclosed the existence of the "talking points" memo, at its online site, reporting it was "not clear who prepared these talking points, but Starr believes that Lewinsky did not write them herself. He is investigating whether the instructions came from (Vernon) Jordan or other friends of the President."

2) On **1/22**, *NBC News at Sunrise* reported, "prosecutors suspect the President and his longtime friend, Vernon Jordan, tried to cover up allegations that Mr. Clinton was involved sexually with White House

intern Monica Lewinsky and other women—which is why this document, obtained last night by NBC News, could be a smoking gun. It's called, 'Points to make in affidavit.'"

3) On **1/ 24,** *US News Online* published a version of the "talking points" containing the line: "You have never observed the President behaving inappropriately with anybody." It was the only version that would have the line.

4) On **2/2,** *USA Today* reported that Lindsey disavowed any responsibility for the "talking points."

5) In *US News's* **2/2** issue, an editor's note reported that the version posted was "only the first page and parts of the second page...(and) that the copy we were given was retyped at least once....That could account for minor typographical differences of the "talking points" published by different news organizations."

6) On **2/4**, the *NBC Nightly News*, referring to the "talking points" memo, reported "Sources in Starr's office and close to Linda Tripp say they believe the instructions came from the White House. If true, that could help support a case of obstruction of justice."

7) On **2/5**, the *Washington Post* reported that in a proffered statement to the prosecutors "Lewinsky did not discuss the origins of one of the crucial pieces of evidence in the investigation—the so-called talking points. . . . Sources said that Ginsburg had told prosecutors that Lewinsky was prepared to provide a full version of events—including the origin of the talking points—if an agreement was concluded based on her statement."

8) On **2/5,** *USA Today* ran a slightly different version of the memo.

9) On **2/6,** *USA Today* reported "Starr's investigators are exploring whether anyone close to Clinton prepared or knew about the talking points."

10) On **2/8,** the *New York Times* ran another slightly different version of the memo.

11) In its **2/9** issue, *Time* said that in his appearance before the grand jury, "potentially the most damaging questions for Lindsey will concern the list of 'talking points' that Lewinsky allegedly gave Linda

Tripp in mid-January, shortly before Tripp was scheduled to give a deposition in the Paula Jones case. ...The origins of the talking points remain a big mystery, but Starr may have good reason to press Lindsey under oath."

12) On **2/10,** the *Washington Post* ran yet another slightly different version of the memo's text along with analysis of it and interviews with lawyers who "concluded that the document may have a lawyer's hand behind it."

13) On **2/19,** the *New York Times* reported "It is unclear who wrote the talking points and whether they were given to Ms. Tripp on Jan. 14 to encourage her to give false testimony in the Paula Corbin Jones sexual misconduct lawsuit against the President. These are questions of intense interest to Independent Counsel Kenneth W. Starr, said lawyers close to his investigation....The talking points could be an important piece of physical evidence showing that there were unlawful efforts to encourage false testimony in the Jones case....Whether the genesis of the somewhat clumsily crafted talking points memorandum will ever be known is unclear."

14) On **2/19,** *CNN* confused matters when they used the term "talking points" to describe an altogether different memo Lewinsky had told Tripp she had taken off her boss Ken Bacon's desk, about an overseas journey by the President. CNN said, "Sources independent of the investigation who took notes while listening to the secretly recorded tapes tell CNN Lewinsky stole what she described as the 'talking points' to try to position herself to be on the trip. Lewinsky's lawyer is denouncing release of this information."

15) On **2/23,** *Fox News Special* reported "according to sources" Starr's team is "considering the possibility that President Clinton helped Monica Lewinsky write the so-called 'talking points' memo" because they met at the White House on Dec. 27, "just a few weeks before Lewinsky gave Linda Tripp the memo."

16) On **3/7,** the *New York Times* reported, "Based largely on two pieces of evidence—those talking points and the secret tapes made by Mrs. Tripp of her conversations with Ms. Lewinsky—Mr. Starr is trying to determine whether the President, Mr. Jordan, Ms. Lewinsky or others set about to obstruct justice in the Jones case by lying, concealing evidence, and tampering with witnesses."

17) On **3/10,** the *Washington Post* reported, "Because of Lindsey's earlier discussions with Tripp about the Willey incident, prosecutors appear to be trying to learn whether he had any role in helping Lewinsky prepare the three-page document. Lindsey, who has been summoned to the grand jury twice, has denied any connection to the 'talking points.'"

18) In its **3/23** issue, *Newsweek* reported Lewinsky appeared to know what Clinton would say in the Kathleen Willey case, that Clinton would be extremely upset if Tripp contradicted him, according to Lewinsky, who added Tripp and her children were "'in danger' if she didn't testify the right way about the Willey episode." Lewinsky then handed Tripp the "talking points," the story said, and that Tripp doubted they had been written by Lewinsky and thought "one part of the talking points seemed to echo the approach, if not the actual words, of Bruce Lindsey."

19) On the **4/19** *This Week*, Tripp lawyer Anthony Zaccagnini denied the "talking points" said, "Please lie about this." "I think the purpose of the talking points was to provide someone a means of communicating certain information without incriminating anyone," he said.

20) On **5/18**, the *Washington Times* reported, "Mr. Starr, according to lawyers and others close to the grand jury probe, wants to know what White House Deputy Counsel Bruce R. Lindsey and senior aide Sidney Blumenthal know about the source of the summary, or 'talking points' that were given to Mrs. Tripp by Miss Lewinsky, the former White House intern. The summary, which prosecutors are convinced was not written by Miss Lewinsky, could corroborate accusations of a White House attempt to obstruct justice and suborn perjury in the Jones suit, sources said."

21) On **6/10**, *Fox News Special* reported, "Fox News has learned investigators working for (Starr) won't consider a deal for immunity until Lewinsky reveals who helped her write the so-called 'Talking points' memo." Fox quoted former Independent Counsel Michael Zeldin: "If you can establish that Vernon Jordan, the President or the President's agents gave these to Monica Lewinsky with the intent to have her improperly influence Linda Tripp to lie, then you've got something there."

22) On **6/11,** the *New York Times* reported "The talking points memorandum and the Tripp-Lewinsky tapes form the backbone of the

independent counsel's inquiry into whether anyone lied or obstructed justice over Ms. Lewinsky's relationship with President Clinton."

23) On *CNBC*, **6/17**, Chris Matthews: ". . . What I think is the toughest nut to crack here, could it be that Monica is not protecting Bruce Lindsey, and not Bob Bennett, not Vernon Jordan, but the person who may have given her the 'talking points' may in fact have been the person she had the closest relationship with, the person who had the closest relationship with her, and that's the President. But if the President gave her the 'talking points,' she can't give him away without bringing down this administration. . . . I'll tell you one thing, if every prosecutor in this country were as tough as Ken Starr, the streets would be swept of criminals right now."

24) On **6/22**, the *Washington Times* reported that Starr "has focused on White House Deputy Counsel Bruce R. Lindsey" as the possible source for the "talking points." "Specifically, the independent counsel's office is trying to gather evidence to bolster the following scenario: Mrs. Tripp relayed her concerns to Miss Lewinsky, who mentioned them to Mr. Clinton. The president then briefed Mr. Lindsey, his closest adviser, who responded by arranging for Miss Lewinsky to give Mrs. Tripp the talking points."

25) On **6/29**, *USA Today* reported "The document has emerged as possible evidence of obstruction of justice as Starr investigates whether Clinton or his associates made attempts to conceal the president's encounters with women."

26) *USA Today* on **7/1** reported that the "talking points" memo might prove to be the most important evidence. The writers quoted "legal experts" saying the "talking points" are "the meat of possible obstruction of justice or witness-tampering charges." They quote Paul Rothstein, law professor at Georgetown University: "The talking points are the closest thing to a smoking gun in this case." With the story is what they describe as "the actual text" of the "talking points."

27) On the **7/6** *CNN Burden of Proof*, English Professor John Gillis discussed his report, co-authored with Skip Fox, on the origin of the "talking points." He believes there were two authors: "Our hypothesis is that it was some lawyer that was working on Linda Tripp's behalf . . . very conscientious, albeit in haste. The second author seems to be some friend or confidante of Linda Tripp, and you can make your own guesses. We believe the most likely candidate would be Lucianne

Goldberg." They speculate she e-mailed parts of the "talking points" to Tripp. In an online report on "The Real News Page" on Sept. 17, Gallagher and Fox asserted that sometime subsequent to this TV appearance Lucianne Goldberg reported her hard drive failed.

28) On **7/27**, the *New York Times* reported "The talking points, which seemed intended to coach Mrs. Tripp in possible testimony about Mr. Clinton, are central to Mr. Starr's effort to determine whether obstruction of justice occurred."

29) On *CNBC* **7/29**, Chris Matthews asked Lucianne Goldberg about the speculation that Lewinsky wrote the "talking points" with ideas from Linda Tripp. "I haven't spoken to Linda about it," she responded, "but I suggest that what happened would be that they were—they were working out what they were going to do about the Willey situation, who was going to say what. And Linda said, 'well, if you want to know what I say about it, go and read the letter I wrote to Newsweek last summer.' So Monica toodles off, gets that language and incorporates it into her typing."

30) On **7/29**, the *NewsHour with Jim Lehrer* interviewed print reporters on a Starr investigation update segment. The *Time* correspondent reported the "talking points" "to date had been the most tangible possible evidence of obstruction of justice that could have been made in any case against the White House. Now we have Monica Lewinsky saying nobody at the White House helped me write them. . . ."

The Starr Report and supporting documents

The Starr report devotes only one paragraph to the "talking points." It is as follows:

"On January 14, Ms. Lewinsky gave Ms. Tripp a three-page document regarding 'points to make in [Ms. Tripp's] affidavit.' Ms. Lewinsky testified that she wrote the document herself, although some of the ideas may have been inspired by conversations with Ms. Tripp."

There is also a footnote. It reads: "Ms. Tripp, in contrast, testified that she believed Ms. Lewinsky received assistance in drafting the talking points."

Appendix 6

Vernon Jordan's Role

The earliest stories often overstated what Lewinsky really told Tripp about whether Vernon Jordan told her to lie about her affair with Clinton. The coverage in the following weeks included Jordan's denials, but tended to maintain that he might be in big trouble despite them. These news accounts also failed to adequately consider that Lewinsky might be exaggerating or misleading about what she told Tripp.

The allegations against Jordan also spawned profiles that often depicted him as an amoral character, included pejorative anecdotes, and emphasized stories about his attitude toward women.

Lewinsky eventually told investigators that on the matter of Jordan's role, she had exaggerated in her comments to Tripp. In the end, the Starr Report omits any mention of either attempted obstruction by Jordan, or the taped allegations of his telling Lewinsky to lie under oath. The other evidentiary materials also proved inconclusive.

A chronology of stories on Jordan's involvement:

1) On Wednesday, **1/21**, the *Washington Post* reported that according to sources Lewinsky told Tripp on tape of "Clinton and Jordan directing her to testify falsely."

2) On **1/21**, *ABC's Good Morning America*, citing a source, said Lewinsky could be heard on a tape claiming the president told her to deny an affair and that Vernon Jordan "instructed her to lie." On the 7:30 segment ABC News reported "that two sources say tapes exist in which" Lewinsky "tells another colleague that" Clinton—and later

his close associate Vernon Jordan—"instructed her to lie under oath about an alleged sexual relationship she had with Clinton. . . . According to a source with a witness familiar in the matter, Lewinsky is heard describing the sexual nature of her relationship with the President. The source says, in another tape Lewinsky claimed she called Mr. Clinton to tell him about the subpoena, and he told her to deny the relationship. On another occasion, Lewinsky allegedly says the President told her he would have Vernon Jordan talk to her. The source says Lewinsky is later heard saying Jordan instructed her to lie, and told her, even if she got caught, they don't prosecute people for lying in civil cases."

3) On **1/21**, the *Los Angeles Times*, in contrast, said simply that Starr was investigating "whether Clinton deployed his friend and trusted advisor, Vernon Jordan, to discuss with Lewinsky her testimony or to otherwise shape her account in the Jones case."

4) On **1/22**, the *Los Angeles Times* reported "If Clinton or friend Vernon Jordan urged her to falsely deny having had a sexual relationship with the president, they could be charged with soliciting perjury and obstruction of justice."

5) On **1/22**, *USA Today* reported "Presidents from Lyndon Johnson to Bill Clinton have relied on good judgment and sound advice from Vernon Jordan. But the latest furor depicts the powerful Georgetown lawyer in an unfamiliar role: contributing to problems instead of solving them." (Starr) "is investigating whether Jordan urged" Lewinsky "to deny the affair and helped her get a job." This is a case, it should be noted, of the press reporting what Starr was investigating or suspecting, not what he knew.

6) On **1/22**, *Newsweek* in its AOL piece noted "However, there was no clear evidence on the (Tripp) tape (which *Newsweek* heard) that would confirm or deny Tripp's allegation that Clinton or Vernon Jordan had coached Lewinsky to lie." The report also said the magazine had "obtained what may be an important new piece of evidence" (the "talking points" memo). "It's not clear who prepared these talking points, but Starr believes that Lewinsky did not write them herself. He is investigating whether the instructions came from Jordan or other friends of the President."

7) On **1/22**, *ABC* featured "A close look at the other man in this White House crisis—Vernon Jordan. He is accused of encouraging Monica

Lewinsky to lie under oath about a sexual relationship she's alleged to have had with the president. This is much more the nub of the crisis than any sex which may have been involved. . . ."

"According to sources who have heard the secret tapes, Monica Lewinsky says Jordan told her to lie about her relationship with the president. . . ."

"Ken Starr would have to prove that Vernon Jordan intended that Monica Lewinsky lie in her deposition. It's very hard to get that kind of state of mind evidence and he doesn't yet."

8) On **1/23**, most news organizations prominently featured Vernon Jordan's public denial in which he said "At no time did I ever say, suggest or intimate to her (Lewinsky) that she should lie," and Jordan's statement that both the President and Lewinsky had denied to him any sexual affair.

9) On **1/24**, Stuart Taylor of the *National Journal* reported Lewinsky "was allegedly pressed to deny the relationship both by Clinton and his friend Vernon Jordan. . . According to a source familiar with Tripp's account, Lewinsky told Tripp that Clinton (and Jordan) had said repeatedly that if only two people were in a room and both deny that anything happened, 'they can never prove it.' . . . And Starr's office is laying the groundwork for a climactic cross-examination of Clinton about whether he orchestrated a cover-up of his alleged affair with Lewinsky. . . ."

10) On the **1/26** *Good Morning America*, *Newsweek*'s Evan Thomas: "We understand from very reliable sources that when Monica Lewinsky was talking to Tripp, her friend, and Tripp was on—being wired Lewinsky by the FBI, Lewinsky did say some very damaging stuff about Jordan; that Jordan said 'Deny it, say it never happened' that he had basically told her to lie. Now that doesn't mean that Jordan did do that. I have to be careful about that. But the FBI—with the FBI listening, Lewinsky said that's what Jordan said to her. . ."

11) On **1/28**, *USA Today* reports that Jordan, "has another connection to Monica Lewinsky besides his old friend, President Clinton. Jordan is a long-time friend of R. Peter Straus, a wealthy New York media executive who is engaged to Lewinsky's mother, Marcia Lewis."

12) On **1/30**, *USA Today* followed up on its report in a short item called "The dog that didn't bite:" saying, "Vernon Jordan had a ready-made explanation for his seemingly suspicious efforts to find Lewinsky a

private-sector job. Marcia Lewis, Lewinsky's mother, is engaged to marry R. Peter Straus, a long-time friend and business associate of Jordan's. These ties give rise to a perplexing question: Why did Jordan fail to mention last week that Lewinsky will soon be the step-daughter of a close friend?"

13) In its **2/2** issue, *Newsweek* carried a profile of Vernon Jordan, which said he and Clinton are, "Southerners who love to work a room, both men love to eat, golf, tell stories—and flirt with women. Their mutual fondness for the ladies is a frequent, if crude, topic of conversation. . . . Is Vernon Jordan's star finally fading? That depends on whether the man who fixes other people's messes can find a way to fix his own."

14) *Time*, in its **2/2** issue, carried a profile of Vernon Jordan which reported, "Lewinsky reportedly told Tripp that Jordan said to her, 'They can't prove anything. . . . Your answer is, It didn't happen, it wasn't me.' If that turns out to be true, Jordan could be on the hook for suborning perjury and obstruction of justice. . . ." The profile quoted Jordan's categorical denial but said that in his statement he was "wrapping himself in a protective layer of syntax." *Time* added, "If Jordan's performance seemed stagy and even sanctimonious, it may have been because 'drive, ambition and personality' are not the only attributes he and Clinton are known to find impressive in young women. 'Large men of large appetites' is one of the euphemisms that have been used when broaching the subject of their legendary womanizing. . . ."

15) On the **2/15** *Sixty Minutes*, Mike Wallace profiled Vernon Jordan emphasizing the theme of President Clinton and Jordan crudely discussing women together.

16) On **2/21**, the *New York Times*, *Newsweek* and *NBC* were reporting on Jordan's version of events—that he did not know of the sexual relationship, which was denied to him by both parties, and he was unaware Lewinsky was the target of an investigation.

17) On the **3/1** *This Week*, *ABC* reported Jordan's version and "that he was acting in total innocence when he went to what some would say were extraordinary lengths to find this young woman a lawyer and a job. Now the tapes suggest a different scenario, that Mr. Jordan was aware that there was something of a sexual nature. . . between the President and Lewinsky, and that he did tell her, or instruct her, or encourage her, to deny there was a relationship when she went under

oath in the Paula Jones case. And that's what the prosecutors will be asking him about."

18) On the **3/1** *Meet the Press*, Sen. Orrin Hatch (R-UT) said, "There is a rumor now that he (Starr) has given limited use immunity to Vernon Jordan."

19) On **3/1**, reacting to Hatch's comment, *ABC* reported: "Vernon Jordan today refused to discuss reports he may be given limited immunity when he appears before the grand jury on Tuesday. Which raises a question—why would Jordan need immunity when he so adamantly denied the most serious accusation concerning Monica Lewinsky's relationship with the President?"

20) On **3/3**, the *Washington Post* reported on Jordan's scheduled appearance before the grand jury that day. The defense Jordan "appears to be establishing for himself . . . hinges on the idea that even if there was a sexual relationship. . . he was an unwitting participant in any cover-up."

21) On **3/3**, the *NewsHour* interviewed Dan Balz of the *Washington Post* who reported, "the tapes that involve Monica Lewinsky and Linda Tripp indicated that Vernon Jordan had asked Monica Lewinsky to lie in the Paula Jones deposition that she was about to give. . . . That's according to people who were familiar with those tapes. They believe that's what she was saying."

22) On **3/3**, Stuart Taylor appeared on *MSNBC's The News*: "I think the speculation that he's going to hurt (Clinton) might be very wrong. . . I think it would be very hard for Vernon Jordan to be put in any jeopardy here. I expect Starr may be trying to make a case that Vernon Jordan was, perhaps, an unwitting tool of a cover up."

Starr Report and supporting documents

The Starr report does not point to any attempted obstruction by Jordan or taped allegations of his urging Lewinsky to lie, saying only that "OIC investigators and prosecutors recognized parallels between Mr. Jordan's relationship with Ms. Lewinsky and his earlier relationship with pivotal Whitewater-Madison figure Webster L. Hubbell."

Contrary to various press accounts detailed here, there is nothing in the Starr report substantiating allegations that Lewinsky said to Tripp that Jordan coached her to lie. After noting Jordan's testimony that "Ms.

Lewinsky said she had not had a sexual relationship with the President," the report states the following: "Ms. Lewinsky testified, however, that at this time she assumed Mr. Jordan knew 'with a wink and a nod' that [she] was having a relationship with the President. She therefore interpreted Mr. Jordan's question as 'What are you going to say,' rather than 'What are the accurate answers.' "

Further the report says, "In January 1998, Linda Tripp, a witness in three ongoing OIC investigations, came forward with allegations that (i) Monica Lewinsky was planning to commit perjury in *Jones v. Clinton*, and (ii) she had asked Ms. Tripp to do the same. Ms. Tripp also stated that (i) Vernon Jordan had counseled Ms. Lewinsky and helped her obtain legal representation in the *Jones* case, and (ii) at the same time, Mr. Jordan was helping Ms. Lewinsky obtain employment in the private sector.

"OIC investigators and prosecutors recognized parallels between Mr. Jordan's relationship with Ms. Lewinsky and his earlier relationship with a pivotal Whitewater-Madison figure, Webster L. Hubbell. Prior to January 1998, the OIC possessed evidence that Vernon Jordan—along with high-level associates of the President and First Lady—helped Mr. Hubbell obtain lucrative consulting contracts while he was a potential witness and/or subject in the OIC's ongoing investigation. . . .

"Against this background, the OIC considered the January 1998 allegations that: (i) Ms. Lewinsky was prepared to lie in order to benefit the President, and (ii) Vernon Jordan was assisting Ms. Lewinsky in the *Jones* litigation, while simultaneously helping her apply for a private-sector job with, among others, Revlon, Inc.

"Based in part on these similarities, the OIC undertook a preliminary investigation. On January 15, 1998 the Office informed the Justice Department of the results of our inquiry. The Attorney General immediately applied to the Special Division of the Court of Appeals for the District of Columbia Circuit for an expansion of the OIC's jurisdiction. The Special Division granted this request and authorized the OIC to determine whether Monica Lewinsky or others had violated federal law in connection with the *Jones v. Clinton* case."

According to the transcript of the FBI sting tape released by the House Judiciary Committee, this is what Lewinsky told Tripp about Vernon Jordan's advice on her sworn affidavit:

Tripp(T): "Did he say anything about—and, now this is—this is touchy and you don't have to answer it."
Lewinsky(L): "Right."
T: "But did he address the perjury issue at all? Because that is perjury."
L: "OK, he—Yeah. He said that—he said, 'You're not gonna go to jail. You're not going to go to jail.'"

T: "You're not going to go to jail, but did he—did he—did he assess what could happen? I mean assuming—let's say worst case, they come up to me or to you and say 'you on this date and this date and this date said something completely wrong to us. It's obviously a falsehood.' And let's just say it's perjury or can be construed as perjury. Did he—"

L: "I would say it's not. What I said is true. It did not happen. She is—I did not say that. She must have misunderstood. Maybe—"

T: "I mean, you're not hearing what I'm saying. I understand all that."

L: "O.K."

L: "I—I—I've gotten that."

L: "See, no. No. I understand what you're saying. What I'm trying to show you is that what he has showed me is there's no way to get caught in perjury in a situation like this."

T: "Really?"

L: "In a situation like this—"

T: "He's sure?"

L: "That's—look that's what he's told me."

T: "When he presented it to you, did he seem sure?"

L: "Yes."

T: "Like—but you don't seem to be concerned about that anyway."

L: "I'm not because—because of all those reasons."

T: "I know. But did you express concern at all?"

L: "Yes, I did. Of course I did."

T: "You said—"

L: "I was crying."

T: "You were?"

L: "Yeah."

T: "O.K. So you knew—he knew that you were concerned."

L: "Yes. Oh, yes."

Appendix 7

Betty Currie

The initial *New York Times* account accurately reported what Currie told investigators about Clinton having "led her through an account of his relationship" with Lewinsky and her retrieving gifts from Lewinsky. The *Times*, however, played in the seventeenth paragraph Currie's response through her attorney.

Subsequent press accounts were less careful than the *New York Times*. The *Times*' painstaking but suggestive wording of Clinton having "led" Currie through questioning had become "coaching" Currie in reports by other outlets. Some commentators leaped to broad conclusions in speculating about what effect Currie and the gifts would have on Clinton's future.

In the end, Starr makes Currie a key part of the impeachment case, but acknowledges that he has conflicting testimony about what happened. Overall, the *New York Times* account, which constituted the principal source for other reporting, holds up well.

A chronology of stories on Betty Currie's involvement:

> On **1/22** the *Los Angeles Times* reported that Lewinsky visited the White House "numerous times in the months after her internship ended, knowledgeable sources said." "They said on each occasion," Lewinsky "was authorized to enter" by Currie.
>
> On **1/22** *Newsweek* on America Online reported that Lewinsky first went to see Jordan at the "instruction" of Currie. And Lewinsky sent packages to the White House using a messenger service. "The contact

number on the packages is . . . the phone number of Clinton's personal secretary, Betty Currie."

On **1/23** the *Washington Post* described Currie as the "genteel gatekeeper" who is "unfailingly gracious." " 'This is not Rose Mary Woods,' "one source said in the piece, "referring to President Richard M. Nixon's secretary who is believed to have erased a key 18 1/2 minutes of the Watergate tapes. 'Betty is not someone who would ever do anything unethical, immoral or untoward. She has made it to where she is because of hard work and because she is just an impeccable woman and not a political hack.' "

On **1/23** an *Associated Press* report carried in the *Chicago Tribune* said her loyalty to Clinton "is undeniable, as is his loyalty to her."

On **1/26** several newspapers ran stories on Currie's character. The *New York Daily News* said aides insist she's not the type to "engage in unseemly wheeling and dealing." The *Los Angeles Times* reported that part of her job as Clinton's personal secretary involves "zealously protecting presidential secrets."

On **1/28** the *Wall Street Journal* reported that Currie "is emerging as a key witness" for Starr because "she appears to have been an important contact" for Lewinsky.

The **2/6** *New York Times* reported that Currie told investigators that Clinton "called her into his office last month and led her through an account of his relationship" with Lewinsky that "differs in one critical aspect from her own recollections, said lawyers familiar with her account." The report also said, "Currie has also retrieved and turned over to investigators several gifts . . . that the president had given Ms. Lewinsky, the lawyers said." Though the account does say "it is not clear who, if anyone, instructed Mrs. Currie to retrieve the gifts," Currie's lawyer's response is stuck deep in the story at the seventeenth graph.

On **2/5**, *Nightline* devoted an entire broadcast to the *Times* report, repeatedly saying they would not be reporting the story if they had not confirmed "essential details" of it with a source themselves. "The essence of this story marks the first time that someone within the president's inner circle is alleging both that Mr. Clinton tried to suggest a particular version of his meetings with Monica Lewinsky and that his version was contrary to what his staffer knew to be true."

Nightline's report refers to a "White House" response, but discounted it as "keeping with the White House strategy to avoid the substance of all these charges."

On **2/5** *MSNBC*, reacting to an early edition of the 2/6 *New York Times*, confirmed the story citing "two source close to the investigation." Appearing on *MSNBC* Deputy Associate Attorney General Bruce Fein comments on the report saying "impeachable offenses don't have to be technical crimes. . . . These are very serious allegations."

On **2/6**, the *Today* show reported that, "[I]n a potentially damaging admission, sources say that Currie has been described being coached by President Clinton as to how she might explain his relationship with Monica Lewinsky."

On the morning of **2/6,** *CNN* reports Currie's attorney Lawrence Wechsler issued this statement: "I am shocked and dismayed by the numerous leaks regarding Mrs. Currie's grand jury testimony. I want to be absolutely clear: To the extent there is any implication or the slightest suggestion that Mrs. Currie believed that the president or anyone else tried to influence her recollection, that is absolutely false and a mischaracterization of the facts."

On **2/6** on its *All Politics* website, *CNN* reported that Currie told Starr's office "she knows of several occasions in which (Clinton and Lewinsky) met alone."

On **2/7** NPR's Nina Totenberg, speaking on *Inside Washington*: "The thing in the story that I think is going to provide the most difficulty for the president is the account that says Betty Currie retrieved from Monica Lewinsky presents that the president had given to her. Now Betty Currie, through her attorney, has said the *New York Times* has mischaracterized her testimony. But you can't mischaracterize presents. And if the Independent Counsel can show that those presents were retrieved on orders from Mr. Clinton, I think that's obstruction of justice."

In its **2/16** issue *Newsweek* reported that Currie "was not just a front-row spectator, but caught up as a player in a high-stakes game." "[D]epending on what she knows and what she is willing to say, she could change the course of Starr's investigation and, possibly, Clinton's presidency." Her role takes the investigation to "new and—for Clinton—dangerous ground." In a different *Newsweek* story in the same issue: "Two key questions come straight from a detective novel: were gifts returned" to the White House? "If so whose idea was it to return them? As a matter of law, if not politics, the president's fate could partly rest on what she knows and what she will eventually say in court."

In its 2/16 issue, *Time* wrote that Currie has " a kind of credibility no one else in this mess could muster. She is a Clinton loyalist, a reluctant witness squeezed between her devotion to her boss and her obligation to the facts. She was "Ken Starr's dream come true."

In its 4/6 issue *Time* reported that, according to an "attorney familiar with the case, . . . even without Lewinsky's direct testimony . . . Congress will have strong circumstantial evidence that suggests Clinton oversaw Lewinsky's job search and tried to coach the testimony of a potential witness," Betty Currie.

Starr Report and supporting documents

On Clinton "coaching" Currie's testimony:

The report says Clinton was never able to "devise an innocent explanation" for why he called Currie into his office for the discussion of past events, discounting his explanation that he was trying to "refresh his memory." It adds that "if the most reasonable inference from the president's conduct is drawn—that he was attempting to enlist a witness to back up his false testimony from the day before—his behavior with Ms. Currie makes complete sense."

On Currie collecting the gifts Clinton had given Lewinsky:

The report says there is conflicting testimony on the gifts. Lewinsky testified that a few hours after she had spoken with the President about the gifts on Dec. 28, 1997, she received a call from Currie saying "'I understand you have something to give me.' Or, 'The President said you have something to give me'—[Something] [a]long those lines."

The report also says that Currie testified that Lewinsky, not Currie, placed the call and raised the subject of transferring the gifts. Currie has testified that Lewinsky said that she (Lewinsky) was uncomfortable holding the gifts because people were asking questions about them. Currie, however, admitted her recollection of events may not have been clear.

The report concludes that Lewinsky's testimony is more reliable than Currie's, but adds that even if Lewinsky "is mistaken" and Currie's chronology is correct, "the evidence still leads to the conclusion that the President orchestrated this transfer."

Appendix 8

Third Party Witnesses

From the earliest days of the story, reports were widely published both that there were third party witnesses who had observed Clinton and Lewinsky in acts of intimacy, or, somewhat more cautiously, that Starr was reaching out to such potential eyewitnesses. Several stories went so far as to name potential eyewitnesses.

Some subsequent reports included not-so-veiled warnings to Lewinsky that if she didn't agree to cooperate soon, Starr wouldn't need her much longer. Neither the Starr Report nor other supporting documents establish any eyewitnesses to acts of intimacy.

Two serious problems are potentially raised here. One is that the press got ahead of the facts because it relied on secondhand sources. The other is that the press was being used by investigative or prosecutorial sources who wanted to employ the media to apply pressure on Lewinsky or other potential witnesses.

A chronology of stories concerning the "third party witness":

> On **1/25**, ABC's *This Week* reported: "ABC News has learned that Ken Starr's investigation has moved well beyond Monica Lewinsky's claims and taped conversations that she had an affair with President Clinton. Several sources have told us that in the Spring of 1996 the President and Lewinsky were caught in an intimate encounter in a private area of the White House. It is not clear whether the witnesses were Secret Service agents or White House Staff. . . . This development . . . underscores how Ken Starr is collecting evidence and witnesses to build a case against the President—a case that would not hinge entirely on the word of Monica Lewinsky." Sam Donaldson

treated the report as a fact and sought comment on it from the show's guest, Rep. Henry Hyde. Hyde declined to comment on the report, calling it "an allegation." And at the conclusion of the show, Donaldson again mentioned the report, saying, "Corroborating witnesses have been found who caught the president and Miss Lewinsky in an intimate act in the White House."

On **1/26**, the *New York Post* and the *New York Daily News* bannered the Sunday *ABC* report with front pages that said "CAUGHT IN THE ACT." The *St. Louis Post-Dispatch* and others carried front page stories attributed to ABC News saying Clinton and Lewinsky were caught in an intimate encounter.

On **1/26**, *ABC* changed the Sunday report on *Good Morning America*, saying that several sources said Starr was "investigating claims that in the Spring of 1996 the President and Lewinsky were discovered in an intimate encounter" and that shortly afterward, Lewinsky was moved out of the White House to the Pentagon. The network also carried White House Press secretary Mike McCurry's sweeping denial of the earlier ABC report.

On **1/26**, *CBS News* reported that sources say Starr is investigating reports of White House staffers who saw Clinton and Lewinsky alone together at various places in the mansion, "including the White House theater and a study off the Oval office."

On **1/26,** the *Washington Post* reported Starr's office would seek to interview Secret Service agents to ask if they personally observed Clinton and Lewinsky engaged in any "intimate acts."

On **1/26,** the *Dallas Morning News* website reported and then, hours later, retracted a report that a Secret Service agent would testify he saw Clinton and Lewinsky in a compromising situation. Before the retraction, *MSNBC* and *CNN's Larry King Live* carried the report and speculated on its consequences. *Nightline* also had carried the report.

On **1/27**, the print edition of *Dallas Morning News* reported "an intermediary for one or more witnesses who report having seen an ambiguous incident involving" Clinton and Lewinsky and who were talking about possible cooperation with Starr.

On **1/28**, *NBC News* quoted "legal sources" saying a Secret Service agent claimed to have seen Lewinsky and Clinton in "unusual circumstances" but Williams added, "the Secret Service insists it knows of no agent who witnessed any compromising behavior involving the President."

On **2/3**, *CBS News* reported "the Secret Service has conducted an internal inquiry and now believes that no agents saw any liaison between the President and Monica Lewinsky."

On **2/4**, the *Wall Street Journal website* reported that White House Steward Bayani Nelvis testified before the grand jury that he saw Clinton and Lewinsky together in the White House, and that he found a stained tissue afterwards. Bureau Chief Alan Murray then told the story on *CNBC*.

In its **2/5** edition the *Wall Street Journal* changed its story to say Nelvis had told this not to the grand jury but to Secret Service agents because he was personally offended when he "found and disposed of tissues with lipstick and other stains on them following a meeting between" Clinton and Lewinsky.

On **2/9**, the *Wall Street Journal* retracted its story and reported Nelvis was questioned for three hours during two grand jury appearances and said he didn't see Clinton alone with Lewinsky.

On **2/11**, the *Washington Post* reported that former Secret Service officer Lewis Fox said that Clinton and Lewinsky "spent at least 40 minutes alone" while Fox was posted outside the Oval Office door. "She had arrived with papers for the president, he said, and Clinton instructed Fox to usher her into his office," the account said. "[H]is statement could be critical to independent counsel Kenneth Starr's attempt to determine whether" Clinton and Lewinsky had a relationship and tried to conceal it.

In its **4/6** issue, *Time* reported Starr had set his sight on two eyewitnesses. One is a Secret Service agent who has told colleagues he saw Clinton and Lewinsky in a compromising situation. The second is Lewinsky herself.

On **4/14**, *ABC* reported that "sources" said Starr had "subpoenaed seven Secret Service uniformed guards to find out what they know of the Clinton-Lewinsky relationship, and that Starr believes Bayani Nelvis, the steward, did indeed tell some of these agents he found lipstick-stained towels in the Oval Office study after a Clinton-Lewinsky meeting." *ABC* added, "But a lawyer close to the case says that Nelvis has denied the story to the grand jury."

On **7/7,** *ABC* reported that the Federal Appeals Court had ruled that Secret Service agents must testify in Starr's case. The report said, "This decision means that Ken Starr could have access to witnesses who could have seen something between the President and Monica Lewinsky, instead of just having heard of their alleged relationship."

On **7/17,** Starr said publicly that the Office of Independent Counsel "is in possession of information that Secret Service personnel may have observed evidence of possible crimes while stationed in and around the White House." The *Los Angeles Times* quoted Michael Leibig, attorney for some agents: "The areas that he's (Starr's) interested in, I think, are much more specific than some of the press stories have been. They're not generally 'Did you see a crime?' They're generally 'On January 23, where were you, where were other people?' "

By **7/19,** many news organizations were reporting, based on named sources representing the subpoenaed agents, that no agent claimed to have seen Clinton and Lewinsky in a compromising position, but several would testify they saw Lewinsky join Clinton alone in the Oval Office for periods of private time.

Starr Report and supporting documents

The Starr Report is mute on the quest for third party witnesses to the Clinton-Lewinsky meetings. It does, however, use the testimony of the Secret Service agents to build the case that Lewinsky's version of the affair is credible because these witnesses saw her arrive in the President's office.

And the supporting documents to the Starr Report show that Secret Service agent Gary J. Byrne testified steward Bayani Nelvis told him about lipstick-stained towels that the President had left in his study, and that Nelvis complained he was tired of cleaning up that stuff. Byrne said he thought the stains had been left by another woman who worked in the White House, not Monica Lewinsky, and that he suggested to Nelvis the steward should discard the towels rather than send them to the White House laundry where they might "give anybody any more fuel for any more rumors about the President."

Byrne testified that agent John Muskett told him of discovering Clinton and Lewinsky in a compromising moment. Muskett denies it.

Appendix 9

"The Second Intern"

The discussion of other women surfaced almost immediately, first by pundit Ann Coulter on CNBC's *Rivera, Live!* and then Internet columnist Matt Drudge, who was asked about it on NBC's *Meet the Press.*

The allegation remained dormant until August, when Chris Matthews on CNBC and Fred Barnes of the *Weekly Standard* on Fox News renewed the rumors. That spawned coverage in the *New York Post* and elsewhere.

There is no evidence supporting a second intern, or anyone else, in the Starr Report or in the evidentiary material. Kathleen Willey's account stands apart from this thread, as her accusation came from her own lips detailed in a *60 Minutes* broadcast.

A Chronology of the Second Intern rumor:

1) On Friday, **1/23**, two days after the Lewinsky story broke. Ann Coulter, a regular panelist on the CNBC show *Rivera, Live!* was asked by Geraldo Rivera if she thought it was "sleazy" that Monica Lewinsky was detained by the prosecutors for "eight to nine hours without an attorney present." She responded it was not as bad as "the President of the United States using her to service him, along with four other interns."

2) On the **1/25** *Meet the Press*, host Tim Russert asked Matt Drudge about reports that on the tapes there are "discussions of other women, including other White House staffers involved with the President." Drudge replied, "There is talk all over this town another White House staffer is going to come out from behind the curtains this week . . . there are hundreds, hundreds, according to Miss Lewinsky, quoting Clinton. . . ."

3) On **8/28,** on *CNBC's Hardball* Chris Matthews interviewed Lucianne Goldberg and asked her if she had hard evidence that more than one young intern was involved. Goldberg responded, "No, not an intern. I know there were other women that were on the staff that were involved....These were women who were actively involved. It's all going to come out."

4) On **8/30,** on the *Fox News Channel's The Beltway Boys*, co-host Fred Barnes of the *Weekly Standard* told viewers: "The second intern. Politicians, newspaper reporters, TV people all around town were talking about the possibility that there's a second intern who was sexually involved with the President. If there is, that will certainly be dynamite."

5) On **9/2**, the *New York Post* disclosed the rumor to its readers, writing in its "Page Six" gossip column "the Beltway is buzzing" that Bob Woodward of the *Washington Post* is "about to break a big exclusive about a second White House intern." The Post then quoted Woodward as saying the report was "absolutely untrue" and that he had gotten several similar inquiries and had made the same denial.

6) On **9/4**, *WMAL* radio in Washington passed the rumor to its listeners. Radio anchor Andy Parks asked ABC correspondent Bettina Gregory about rumors "that the *Washington Post* is about to go with a story that talks about other interns involved." Gregory responded, "Bob Woodward has denied that, and I don't know whether he denied it because he didn't want other people to work on it. For a long time there have been rumors—this is speculation—unconfirmed rumors that there were other interns that had been involved."

7) On **9/5,** the *Washington Post* published Howard Kurtz's detailed report on the rumor from Barnes' first reference through the *New York Post* and WMAL repetitions of the unsubstantiated rumor.

Starr Report

There is nothing in the Starr Report about the possibility of a second intern or other staff member being involved with the President.

Appendix 10

The Cigar Story

Washington summer gossip included a rumor that Lewinsky had used a cigar as a sex toy while with the President. It started with an internet posting on the *Drudge Report*, was broadcast later the same day by Drudge on his Fox News Channel show, then spread to veiled references on the Sunday talk shows, then to the *London Times*, then to Jay Leno's monologue, then to a column in the *Washington Times* and elsewhere in the mainstream press as references to "kinky sex," including on *Meet the Press* and on one CNN talk program.

In general, however, it is fair to say the press resisted spreading such rumors. The *Drudge Report* turned out to be wrong in some details, as did most of the reports flowing from it. But the Starr Report does include a sentence confirming a Clinton-Lewinsky use of a cigar in a sexual act.

A chronology of the cigar story:

1) On Saturday 8/22, the *Drudge Report* provided details about a particular Clinton-Lewinsky encounter, citing "multiple sources close to the case." In an item headlined, "MEDIA STRUGGLES WITH SHOCKING NEW DETAILS OF WHITE HOUSE AFFAIR," he wrote:

   "In a bizarre daytime sex session, that occurred just off the Oval Office in the White House, President Clinton watched as intern Monica Lewinsky masturbated with his cigar. It has been learned that several major news organizations have confirmed the shocking episode and are now struggling to find ways to report the full Monica Lewinsky/Bill Clinton grossout.

"Media Bigfeet are trying to reconstruct one sex session that reportedly took place as Yasser Arafat waited in the Rose Garden for his scheduled meeting with the president.

"According to multiple sources close to the case, President Clinton allegedly masturbated as Lewinsky performed the sex show with his cigar in a small room off the Oval Office. It is not clear if Clinton kept the cigar, or if Lewinsky testified on the specifics of the encounter before a federal grand jury this week."

2) On his *Fox News Channel* show on **8/22**, Matt Drudge hinted at the account's contents, sanitizing them for television. "So what are these salacious details that journalists are wrestling with this weekend?" Drudge said. "Let's just say one episode allegedly involves a cigar. And I've learned they weren't smoking it."

3) On Sunday **8/23**, various news show guests mentioned the Drudge account, while not specifically discussing it. "Well, I mean, if you read the paper this morning . . . of what he made this poor girl do," said Jerry Falwell on *CNN's Both Sides With Jesse Jackson*. Mary Matalin on *Meet the Press*, "We all know inside the Beltway what's in that report. And I don't think [Clinton] wants his family to know any more about what's in the report, or the country needs to hear any more about tissue, dresses, cigars, ties, anything else."

4) Monday **8/24**, *The (London) Times* cited the *Drudge Report* in its pages: "Matt Drudge the Internet columnist who revealed the Lewinsky affair on his Website, alleged at the weekend that the President and the trainee [Monica Lewinsky] engaged in a sex act involving a cigar." The Hotline also began fully reporting the reporting on the story.

5) On the Monday evening, **8/24**, Jay Leno cryptically joked about the story on the *Tonight Show* no less than five times: "You know who I saw this weekend? Monica Lewinsky. She was ahead of me in line at the cigar store. . . . I'm still trying to figure out how we can even talk about this stuff on a non-cable show," Leno said.

6) On Tuesday **8/25,** the *New York Post* ran a short Page Six item, discussing how news editors were wrestling with reports of the "kinkiest sex act" Clinton "enjoyed" with Lewinsky.

7) In his **8/26** media column, the *Washington Post's* Howard Kurtz wrote that, "the mainstream media, meanwhile, are grappling with

how to deal with the seamier details of the affair. . . . In recent days, cyber-gossip Matt Drudge has alleged a kinky sexual episode that would further tarnish the president's image." He then went on to list other media mentions of the Drudge account.

8) In his **8/28** column, the *Washington Times*' Wesley Pruden wrote: "Never have so many jokes been made about the president's cigar, the phallic toy that Monica is said to have employed in the pantry to the president's delighted applause. . . . The mainstream newspapers, including this one, have avoided saying exactly what it was the president suggested Miss Lewinsky do with his cigar, though everyday they skate closer to the explanation, as if one were needed."

9) On **8/29**, the *Houston Chronicle* published a column by Susan Estrich lamenting the cigar episode, blaming the *Drudge Report* to the Leno circuit.

10) On **8/30**, the *Denver Post* in a piece headlined "The Sordid, Shameful Details" reported: "According to an Aug. 22 Drudge Report published on the Internet, Clinton and Lewinsky indulged in a lewd and lascivious daytime sex session, conducted in a small room off the oval office, involving what can best be described in a family newspaper as parallel acts of masturbation. You'll have to read between the lines."

Starr Report and supporting documents

"At one point, the President inserted a cigar into Ms. Lewinsky's vagina, then put the cigar in his mouth and said: 'It tastes good.' (274) After they were finished, Ms. Lewinsky left the Oval Office and walked through the Rose Garden. (275)"

Notes

Chapter 1

1. Norman Ornstein, Thomas Mann, and Michael Malbin, *Vital Statistics on Congress* (Washington, D.C.: American Enterprise Institute—Congressional Quarterly, 1998).
2. Harris Wofford, *Of Kennedys and Kings: Making Sense of the Sixties* (Pittsburgh, Pa.: University of Pittsburgh Press, 1980), p. 204.
3. Rosenstiel interview with Harris Wofford, July 1998.
4. Committee of Concerned Journalists forum transcript, March 4, 1998.
5. Walter Lippmann, *Liberty and the News* (New Brunswick, N.J.: Transaction, 1995[1920]), pp. 52–53.

Chapter 2

1. Steven Brill, "Pressgate," *Brill's Content*, August 1998, p. 125.
2. *Newsweek*'s doubts about running the story and its resulting decision not to contact the White House for comment until Saturday or beyond had several interesting effects. One noteworthy fact was that the president went to the deposition in the Paula Jones case on Saturday with no awareness that the Justice Department was investigating a possible affair with Lewinsky based on audiotape recordings of Lewinsky, that *Newsweek* knew it, and that Jones's attorneys were fully aware of it.

3. Tom Rosenstiel, "Intercom for Capitol: Sunday TV Shows Play a Subtle Role," *Los Angeles Times,* October 27, 1985, p. A1.

4. Committee of Concerned Journalists forum transcript, February 18, 1998.

5. Brill, p. 134.

6. ABC *This Week*, January 25, 1998.

7. Russell Baker, "The Media in Trouble," *New York Times*, January 30, 1998, p. 17.

8. Committee of Concerned Journalists forum transcript, March 27, 1988.

CHAPTER 3

1. *Analysis* here is defined as an interpretative statement from a journalist that he or she attributes to some sourcing or reporting so that the audience can evaluate its credibility. This accounted for 23 percent of all reportage. *Opinion* is defined as an interpretation by a journalist that is not attributed to anything—just "I think." *Speculation* is an opinion about facts that have not happened yet or that the reporter cannot know—a hypothetical question. *Judgment* is defined as a flat and unequivocal statement, such as, "the president will have to resign if he is lying."

2. Committee of Concerned Journalists study released February 18, 1998, "The Clinton Crisis and the Press: A New Standard of American Journalism?" p. 1 (see Appendix 1).

3. Committee of Concerned Journalists study released March 27, 1998, "The Clinton Crisis and the Press: A Second Look," p. 1 (see Appendix 2).

4. Story thread material comes from the third Committee of Concerned Journalists study, "The Clinton/Lewinsky Story: How Accurate? How Fair?" (see Appendixes 3 through 10).

5. Rosenstiel interview with *New York Times* Washington Bureau Chief Michael Oreskes, March 1998.

CHAPTER 4

1. Perhaps the most typical exception to the two-source rule in those days was that if the source was a principal speaking to reporters in a group, such as when Secretary of State Henry Kissinger briefed reporters on his

airplane about his policy thoughts, he would be described on a background basis. This, generally, is a far different context from the use of anonymous sources in investigative work, where a source's account was treated as a tip until it was verified.

2. Committee of Concerned Journalists study released March 27, 1998, "The Clinton Crisis and the Press: A Second Look," p. 1.

3. Ibid.

4. Ibid.

5. Ibid.

6. Ibid., p. 10.

7. Committee of Concerned Journalists forum transcript, March 27, 1998.

8. Ibid.

9. Jorgen Westerstahl and Folke Johansson, Swedish researchers, found in a 1986 study that the press in that country often sought negative comments from sources and used the comments as a way to ferry negative content into their pieces.

10. Committee of Concerned Journalists forum transcript, March 27, 1998.

11. Committee of Concerned Journalists forum transcript, February 18, 1998.

12. Committee of Concerned Journalists forum transcript, March 27, 1998.

13. Ibid., p. 15.

CHAPTER 5

1. Committee of Concerned Journalists forum transcript, March 27, 1998, p. 15.

2. Roone Arledge speech at the Radio Television Correspondents Association dinner, March 1998.

3. Committee of Concerned Journalists forum transcript, March 27, 1998.

4. Steven Brill, "Pressgate," *Brill's Content*, August 1998, p. 124.

5. Ibid., p. 129; interviews with *Newsweek* staff by Dante Chinni.

6. Rosenstiel interview with a U.S. senator, on a background, not-for-attribution basis, December 1997.

7. Committee of Concerned Journalists forum transcript, December 4, 1997, p. 35.

8. Ibid.

9. Rosenstiel interview with political aide, on a background, not-for-attribution basis, June 1998.

10. Starr filed an emergency motion before the Court of Appeals for the District of Columbia seeking to stay Judge Johnson's "show cause" order. This motion was heavily censored before release but contains the following argument against a hearing to disclose the OIC's contacts with the news media:

[Censored] "It is impossible to disclose the Government's contacts and communications [Censored] without revealing confidential investigative information.

[Censored] ("Long recognized at common law, the informer's privilege serves important individual and societal interests in protecting the anonymity of citizens who cooperate in law enforcement.") Subsequently, Timothy J. Burger of the *N.Y. Daily News* quoted "legal sources outside the prosecutor's office familiar with the proceedings" as confirming that Starr argued "he wanted to keep confidential the information received from reporters, and their identities."

11. The leaks investigation continues under a shroud of secrecy. Judge Johnson has appointed a special master to hear evidence but has not disclosed the master's identity.

12. Soon-to-be published survey of journalists conducted by the Committee of Concerned Journalists during the fall and winter of 1998.

13. The release of the *Starr Report* itself may raise questions about disclosure of grand jury secrets. The *Starr Report* was delivered to the House Judiciary Committee the afternoon of September 9. Officials immediately placed everything under lock and posted armed guards. No member of the House had access to it. Yet the next morning, details of the *Starr Report* appeared in newspapers across the country. The stories cited as sources "lawyers familiar with the report" (*New York Times*), "allies of Mr. Starr" (*Wall Street Journal*), and "sources close to the case" (*Washington Post*). At the time, only the Office of Independent Counsel knew what was in the *Starr Report.* If Starr's office briefed the press before the House decided to release the material, some might argue that constitutes another prima facie violation of Rule 6(e) comparable to those cited earlier by Judge Johnson. The material was grand jury material. Starr's mandate allowed him to deliver it to the House, but Rule 6(e) of the federal Rules of Criminal Procedure still applied to Starr in his dealings with the press and the public. House officials, not subject to Rule 6(e), publicly released the material September 11, two days after stories describing the material appeared.

14. The *Washington Post* and the *New York Times* did occasional stories on the leaks controversy. On February 6, the *NewsHour with Jim Lehrer* devoted a long segment to "the battle over leaks and unnamed sources." On September 30, the *NewsHour* did a long piece on anonymous sources, which featured prominent print journalists.

CHAPTER 6

1. Committee of Concerned Journalists forum transcript, March 27, 1998.

2. Elizabeth Shogren, Richard A. Serrano, and David Willman, "Clinton Enlists Kantor, Offers Specific Denial," *Los Angeles Times*, January 25, 1988, p. 1.

3. *Brill's Content*, August 1998, p. 141, verified by interview by one of this article's authors with a *Times* reporter involved in the story.

4. Janny Scott, "The President Under Fire: Media Notebook; Rules in Flux: News Organizations Face Tough Calls on Unverified 'Facts'," *New York Times*, January 27, 1998, p. 13.

5. Michael Tackett and Roger Simon, "Clinton's Friends Leap to His Defense," *Chicago Tribune*, January 26, 1998, p. 1.

6. Walter Lippmann, *Liberty and the News* (New Brunswick, N.J.: Transaction, 1995[1920]), p. 44.

7. Interviews with several *New York Times* reporters and editors by the authors, March 1998.

8. Committee of Concerned Journalists forum transcript, February 18, 1998, p.12

9. Pew Research Center for the People and the Press Survey, "Event Driven News Audiences, Internet News Takes Off," June 8, 1998, p. 3.

10. Committee of Concerned Journalists forum, February 18, 1998.

11. Howard Kurtz, "Wall Street Journal Story Rushed onto the Web; Response Follows, Disputed Report Is Softened," *Washington Post*, February 5, 1998, p. A12.

12. Committee of Concerned Journalists forum transcript, April 23, 1998.

CHAPTER 7

1. Committee of Concerned Journalists study released February 18, 1998, "The Clinton Crisis and the Press: A New Standard of American Journalism?" p. 1.

2. Committee of Concerned Journalists study released March 27, 1998, "The Clinton Crisis and the Press: A Second Look," p. 3.

3. Steven Brill, "Pressgate," *Brill's Content*, August 1998, p. 133.

4. Rosenstiel interview with Larry Kramer, March 1989.

5. Brill, p. 134.

6. Rosenstiel interviews with Woodward, 1993; Brownstein, 1989.

7. John Podhoretz at the *New York Post* and Bill Kovach at the Nieman Foundation were among those who had come to doubt Glass's work.

8. Rosenstiel interview with writers and editors at *Congressional Quarterly*, February 9, 1999.

9. Committee of Concerned Journalists forum transcript, February 18, 1998.

10. Committee of Concerned Journalists, "The Clinton Crisis and the Press," p. 4: Only 17 percent of the time did reporters name a source for this conclusion. Eleven percent of the time it was cited to another media source.

11. Ibid.

12. Pew Research Center for the People and the Press, survey, "Scandal Reporting Faulted for Bias and Inaccuracy, Popular Policies and Unpopular Press Lift Clinton Ratings," February 6, 1998, question 16.

13. Report on network profitability prepared for the Committee of Concerned Journalists by *Fortune* magazine writer Marc Gunther, based on public profit reports and interviews with NBC executives conducted by Gunther.

14. Howard Kurtz, "The Blond Flinging Bombshells at Clinton; Pundit Is Conservative in Politics Only," *Washington Post*, October 16, 1998, p. D1.

15. Ann Coulter, *High Crimes and Misdemeanors: The Case Against Bill Clinton* (Washington, D.C.: Regnery, 1998), p. 106.

16. Dante Chinni, "Of Human Bombast: Chris Matthews Is a Talking Headcase," *Capital Style*, February 1999, p. 13.

17. Chinni interview with Chris Matthews, December 1998.

18. Tom Rosenstiel, "Reporters on TV: Is Stardom Weakening the Press?" *Los Angeles Times*, April 26, 1989, p. A1.

19. Ibid.

20. Chinni, p. 14.

21. Ibid.

22. Chinni interview with Keith Olberman, December 1998.

23. Felicity Barringer, "In Washington, Is There News After Scandal?" *New York Times*, February 15, 1999, p. D1.

24. Ibid.

25. Lisa de Moraes, "MSNBC's New Right Angle: North and McLaughlin," *Washington Post*, January 28, 1999, p. C7.

26. Pew Research Center survey, February 1997.

27. Charles Krauthammer, "Dog Days in the Golden Age," *Washington Post*, December 19, 1997, p. A25.

28. Committee of Concerned Journalists forum transcript, March 27, 1998.

29. Walter Lippmann, *Liberty and the News* (New Brunswick, N.J.: Transaction, 1995[1920]), pp. 50–51.

CHAPTER 8

1. Pew Research Center survey, "Popular Policies and Unpopular Press Lift Clinton Ratings," February 6, 1998.

2. Rosenstiel interview with Howard Kurtz, December 1998.

3. Rosenstiel interview with journalist Ronald Brownstein of the *Los Angeles Times*, February 1999.

4. In a speech on August 21, 1987, Senator Ted Kennedy attacked Bork and the GOP for the party's trying to change America into a nation under the "rule of Oliver North." Kennedy told a crowd gathered at Citizen Action's Midwest Academy Retreat, "Robert Bork is wrong on civil rights, wrong on equal rights for women, wrong on anti-trust laws, wrong on the First Amendment and wrong on the one-man, one-vote."

5. Robert Berdahl, speech to the American Society of Newspaper Editors' Credibility Think Tank Committee, San Francisco, October 8, 1998.

6. Robert Samuelson, "The Attack Culture," *Washington Post*, March 12, 1997, p. A19.

7. R. W. Apple, "What Next? Don't Guess," *New York Times*, December 20, 1998, p. A1.

8. Princeton Survey Research Associates poll numbers showed Clinton's job approval ratings rose from 61 percent in January 1998 to 71 percent in early February 1998.

9. Gallup Surveys, various, 1998; the Polling Report, various, 1998.

10. Starr's approval rating hovered throughout the scandal from 22 percent to 31 percent, according to PSRA research. GOP congressional leaders hovered between 48 percent and 38 percent. Clinton's approval, as noted, was sharply divided between job approval and personal disapproval.

11. Rosenstiel interview, from the *Los Angeles Times*, November 7, 1988, p. 1.

12. Tom Rosenstiel, *The Beat Goes On: President Clinton's First Year with the Media,* a Twentieth Century Fund Perspective on the News Essay (New York: Twentieth Century Fund Press, 1994), p. 30.

13. Tom Rosenstiel, *Strange Bedfellows: How Television and the Presidential Candidates Changed American Politics, 1992* (Westport, Conn.: Hyperion Press, July 1993), p. 139. The author conducted a content study of the *Washington Post* and *New York Times* front page coverage of Bush between June 1 and the Republican convention in mid-August. Of the 417 stories on Bush, only 23 had a decidedly positive tone. More than 300 were negative. The remainder were mixed or neutral.

14. Rosenstiel, *The Beat Goes On*, p. 31.

15. Project for Excellence in Journalism study released March 6, 1998,

"Changing Definitions of News: A Look at the Mainstream Press Over 20 Years," p. 7.

16. Ibid., p. 6.

17. Ibid., p. 3.

18. Tom Rosenstiel, "Editors Back Reporting Hart Allegations: Some Question Methods and Thoroughness of Miami Writers," *Los Angeles Times*, May 6, 1987, sec. A, p. 15.

CHAPTER 9

1. Committee of Concerned Journalists forum transcript, February 18, 1998.

2. Committee of Concerned Journalists forum transcript, October 20, 1998.

3. Sandra Mims Rowe, speech to the American Society of Newspaper Editors annual convention, April 1998.

4. Committee of Concerned Journalists forum transcript, September 28, 1998.

5. Joseph Pulitzer, "Selection from the College of Journalism," *North American Review,* May 1904, republished in *Killing the Messenger: 100 Years of Media Criticism,* edited by Tom Goldstein (New York: Columbia University Press, 1989), p. 199.

6. Charles William Eliot, *The Development of Harvard University Since the Inauguration of President Eliot, 1869–1929*, edited by Samuel Eliot Morison (Cambridge, Mass.: Harvard University Press, 1930), p. lx.

7. Abraham Lincoln, "Speech to the Young Men's Lyceum of Springfield, Illinois," in *The Essential Abraham Lincoln* (Avenel, N.J.: Portland House, 1993), p. 9.

Index

Acknowledgments

More so than is usual with such projects, many people made this book possible. At the top of that list is Dante Chinni, who worked on the studies that helped frame this work, did research and reporting, and worked on the manuscript. He is the unsung hero. Journalist and friend Jim Doyle is also part of the extended family of authors for the intellect and energy he put into examining the press's coverage of the main threads in the Clinton–Lewinsky story. The rest of the staff of the Committee of Concerned Journalists also played a critical role. Amy Mitchell and John Mashek helped guide the research studies, the drafts, and shaped our thinking throughout. Chris Galdieri helped edit the manuscript and did invaluable and constant research. Nancy Anderson managed the office, proved a master copy editor, and made much of what we did possible. Stacy Forster helped with the research. At the Nieman Foundation, Julie Dempster was an unfailing aide in providing research assistance. Lee Ann Brady and her staff at Princeton Survey Research Associates executed the first two content studies of the Lewinsky coverage that are contained in the first and second appendices. Andy Kohut and the staff of the Pew Research Center for the People and the Press shared with us their research and their insights into public attitudes toward the Clinton scandal and the press. Our thanks to the dozens of journalists, as well as scholar Tom Patterson of the Shorenstein Center at Harvard, who gave us their time in conversation or on the panels we organized for journalists to debate the coverage of this story. Finally, we owe a deep debt of gratitude to Rebecca Rimel and Don Kimelman of the Pew Charitable

Trusts, whose personal and financial support made possible the Committee of Concerned Journalists and the Project for Excellence in Journalism.

About the Authors

Bill Kovach, a newspaper journalist for thirty years, is curator of the Nieman Foundation for Journalism at Harvard University. He was editor of the *Atlanta Journal and Constitution* from 1986 to 1988, during which the paper was awarded two Pulitzer Prizes. Prior to that, he spent two decades at the *New York Times*, serving as the paper's Washington bureau chief from 1978 to 1986. He also worked as a reporter at the *Nashville Tennessean* and the *Johnson City Press-Chronicle* in Tennessee. His other responsibilities include working as ombudsman for *Brill's Content* magazine, serving on the board of directors of various bodies, from *Harvard Magazine* to the Committee to Protect Journalists. He is also the chair of the Committee of Concerned Journalists. He lives in Boston, Massachusetts, with his wife, Lynne. They have four children and six grandchildren.

Tom Rosenstiel, a long-time press critic, is the director of the Project for Excellence in Journalism, a journalists' group affiliated with Columbia University Graduate School of Journalism, funded by the Pew Charitable Trusts. He was a media critic and correspondent for the *Los Angeles Times* from 1983 to 1995, and chief congressional correspondent at *Newsweek* in 1995 and 1996. He is the author of *Strange Bedfellows: How Television And The Presidential Candidates Changed Politics* and The Century Foundation's *The Beat Goes On: President Clinton's First Year with the Media*. His writing has also appeared in *Esquire*, the *New Republic*, the *Washington Post*, the *New York Times*, the *Columbia Journalism Review,* and elsewhere. He is vice chair of the Committee of Concerned Journalists. He lives in Chevy Chase, Maryland, with his wife, Rima, and their two daughters.